SUBURBAN BURGLARY

SUBURBAN BURGLARY

A Time and a Place
for Everything

By

GEORGE RENGERT, Ph.D.

Criminal Justice Department
Temple University
Philadelphia, Pennsylvania

and

JOHN WASILCHICK

Intergovernmental Affairs
Delaware County
Media, Pennsylvania

CHARLES C THOMAS • PUBLISHER
Springfield • Illinois • U.S.A.

Published and Distributed Throughout the World by

CHARLES C THOMAS • PUBLISHER
2600 South First Street
Springfield, Illinois 62717

© *1985 by* CHARLES C THOMAS • PUBLISHER

ISBN 0-398-05142-9

Library of Congress Catalog Card Number: 85-4794

Printed in the United States of America
Q-R-3

Library of Congress Cataloging in Publication Data

Rengert, George F.
    Suburban burglary.

    Bibliography: p.
    Includes index.
    1. Theft — United States — Prevention. 2. Suburban
crimes — United States — Prevention. I. Wasilchick, John.
II. Title.
HV6658.R46 1985   643'.16   85-4794
ISBN 0-398-05142-9

DEDICATION

For Ralph and Edna Rengert who gave their children an important gift, a love for education.

George F. Rengert

For my grandfather, Charles E. Johnston, of Cushing, Oklahoma, for his lesson in perseverance and determination.

John Wasilchick

ACKNOWLEDGMENTS

Many people have contributed to this research. One individual stands out because his help, guidance and encouragement made this book possible. We would like to recognize and thank Mr. Vince Guarini. As Deputy Warden at Delaware County Prison, he not only allowed us to visit and interview prisoners, but he also took the time to make sure we understood what we were doing. His comments and insights gave us a head start in collecting data. He also made sure we knew how the prison operated so that we would understand the ground rules and fit into the routine rather than stand out. We were both pleased, but not surprised, when he was appointed Warden of the Lancaster County Prison not long after we began our work.

CONTENTS

Page

CHAPTER I: INTRODUCTION   3

CHAPTER II: THE USE OF TIME IN BURGLARY 20

CHAPTER III: THE USE OF SPACE IN BURGLARY 53

CHAPTER IV: THE TECHNIQUES OF BURGLARY 76

CHAPTER V: SUBURBAN HOUSING, LIFESTYLE
            AND BURGLARY 104

CHAPTER VI: FINAL THOUGHTS 113

Bibliography 115

Index 121

SUBURBAN BURGLARY

CHAPTER I

INTRODUCTION

BURGLARY is a very common event. Every day in every community someone breaks into someone else's house, steals their possessions, damages their property, and seemingly is never caught. The victim's initial outrage usually subsides into a deep sense of psychological violation. Their dearest and most meaningful possessions are stolen or vandalized, never to be restored. It is an empty feeling. The victim's helplessness is only amplified when the local police confess the truth: nothing can be done. Seldom is the criminal caught and property is almost never recovered.

A great deal of time and effort has been devoted to understanding burglary. Scholars have analyzed and studied it. Criminal justice professionals have suggested many useful ideas to prevent it. Security experts have devised alarm and protective systems that range from simple locks to lasers. Local citizens organize and patrol their neighborhoods. Suburban police departments are usually totally frustrated by burglary. Occasionally, a burglar is caught and prosecuted. No matter what local changes are occurring, the general condition of burglary as a common event remains (Hindelang, Gottfredson and Garofalo, 1978). Its occurrence is all too close to each of us.

Our interest in burglary is somewhat different. We are less concerned with who is likely to commit a burglary than with how to make the burglary process more difficult for any burglar. This is not to demean the efforts of others who are attempting to identify criminogenic persons and situations. They have different priorities and obligations, and their interests reflect this. Our interests began to shift after reading much (and writing some) of the descriptive literature on burglary and burglars, and realizing that we had nothing new to contribute. Our interests are not the same (Rengert, 1975; 1981; Rengert and Wasilchick, 1980).

Our fascination with the process of burglary began when we looked at police incident reports of burglaries and wondered why one house was burglarized and not the one next door or across the street. All seemed equally likely. Every victim must wonder "why me," and we became very curious about the burglar's side of this question. We also wondered about the communities which burglars preferred and why some communities are chosen over others. This is not a transparent question. Suburban counties are usually economically diverse. They are an economic smorgasbord that includes wealthy neighborhoods, distressed ghettos, and areas of every other economic description (Muller, 1981). Given this diversity, we wondered what process really led to the burglary of a single house in a specific neighborhood. How does a burglar discriminate between individual areas and targets when there are so many alternatives to accept and reject?

The burglary of a particular house in a particular neighborhood requires choices, evaluations, motives, some idea of what to do and how to do it, and nerve from the burglar (Jackson, 1969; Walsh, 1980). We had no way of knowing what factors led up to the burglary and how the lives of the home's residents interacted with the life of the burglar (Cohen and Felson, 1979). Once we stopped thinking of burglary as a crime or an isolated event and began to consider it as the result of a process, we realized that the only way to find out more was to ask a burglar.

The idea of asking burglars about burglary was not as far fetched as it might seem. One of us was working for a county court system. This made it easy to telephone the deputy warden and ask how the prison felt about allowing prisoners to be interviewed. The deputy warden also lent the weight of his office to our effort by distributing our request for volunteers and collecting responses through his office. This made the request just official enough to be taken seriously. Our affiliation with Temple University made the request distant enough from the prison administration not to scare away any willing prisoners. The informality of the arrangements worked to our advantage in many unforeseen ways.

We became frequent visitors to this suburban county prison not far from Philadelphia, taking up residence in a small glassed-in room in the netherworld known as the "bullpen." This intermediate area, set off by immense metal gates, lies between the prison inside and the first step out—the prison lobby. The bullpen area has some privacy. It is far enough removed from the distractions of other prisoners and prison activities to hold a normal conversation.

Interviewing Convicted Burglars

Interviewing convicted burglars at the prison was a very surprising experience. The greatest surprise was their willingness to talk at length about their careers. Our greatest fear prior to interviewing was that the burglars would not be willing to say much, be evasive or lie. After our first day of interviewing, we both left the prison shocked by the willingness of burglars to discuss burglary. Our experiences can only be described as contrarian. Most of our preconceived notions of burglars and burglaries were shattered through the course of our early interviews. The interviews were interesting, exciting, and a little frightening. We became so caught up in what we were doing that one day we found ourselves "checking out houses" as we drove away from the prison. We also became acutely aware of our own vulnerability.

There is another side of this experience that frequently muted our enthusiasm. Part of the process of making sense out of our interview data was to verify as much information as possible through public records. These records almost always confirmed at least the outlines of what burglars had told us. Public records often went on to reveal criminal records that included drug abuse and violent crime as well as burglary. This served as a stern reminder that these individuals, no matter how engaging, were still convicted criminals who had committed serious crimes. It was often eerie to discover the darker side of an individual through criminal records. This was especially true when we had found him interesting and polite in an interview the day before. The records available confirmed or lacked information about interview data. Seldom did they refute the burglar's story. The criminal records were always ominous and stark compared to the individual who sat across the table and shared his experiences as a burglar with us.

We interviewed thirty-five individuals over the course of several months. Thirty-one of these gave us information that we were able to use. The other four were not suitable because they were either not burglars (and volunteered anyway) or had no experience or knowledge of the target county. Among these were a pretend gynecologist, a real dentist and a very hostile junkie.

We gathered information from the prisoners about burglaries they had committed, and asked them to explain their method of target selection. We discussed their jobs, friends and families. We asked them to rank order municipalities in the county according to their personal knowledge of the area and the area's potential as a burglary site. We asked questions that would reveal how they conducted burglaries and how these crimes fit into the context of their everyday lives.

The individuals we interviewed formed a diverse group. Each seemed to have his own burglary logic. This is the personal rationale for all the mechanics of the burglary event. Each had his own motives and style. There were nighttime burglars and daytime burglars. Some broke down doors and others used elaborate schemes. This apparent diversity began to dissolve into meaningful patterns of behavior as we began to go beyond the minutiae of mechanics into the general patterns of everyday life. Things became clearer for us when we put burglary into the context of the burglar's everyday life.

These ideas seem straightforward to us now, but they were

arrived at circuitously. Each of the first several interviews pointed our thoughts in a new direction. We had to be fascile in approach and let each individual inform us about what he had to offer. The first interviews were stretched out over several sessions as we modified our approach to accommodate the surprising amount of information the prisoners were willing to give us. We are greatly indebted to these prisoners for educating us in this way. What follows is a description of our experiences, as well as our findings and insights, into the burglary process.

The Burglars

What kind of people are the burglars we interviewed? As a group they were local people. Fifteen of the burglars we interviewed came from the easternmost part of the county, including Upper Darby (3), Darby Borough (3) and Sharon Hill (2). Fifteen came from the Chester City area. Chester City contributed nine burglars, the highest number of any municipality.

They are a young group. More than half (16) are 23 years of age or less. The youngest was 18, although he tried hard to be 17 so that he would be sent to juvenile court. Ten individuals were between 24 and 30 years of age. There were five burglars thirty years and older. The oldest person we interviewed was 35.

Twenty-three of the burglars are white and eight black. Interestingly, the younger burglars, aged 23 or less, are predominantly white (15 of 16). Only one member of the thirty-and-over group is white. All of the burglars who are black come from Chester City (5), Sharon Hill (3), and Upper Darby (1). The white burglars were spread over the areas described above.

While not well educated, there were many intelligent people in this group. Most had employable skills, and many had a trade or craft. Often jobs were quit to pursue burglary full time. The chapter about time will describe some of the problems a full-time job creates for a burglar. Twenty-three had a prior record. Most often prior offenses were for burglary or possession of a controlled substance. There were only a handful with extensive records.

None of these men are alone in the world. Every one had close family ties. Each one had a wife, parents or a sweetheart waiting for him. The best indicators of what the individuals we interviewed are like are their comments and activities presented in the following chapters.

The Study Area: Delaware County

All of this discussion about burglars and burglary may have raised the question, "Just what kind of place is this anyway?" The answer to this question must prevent any misunderstanding about the county we studied and its residents based on our narrow focus on burglars. Delaware County is not a dangerous place with an especially high crime rate (Federal Bureau of Investigation, 1980). Our fascination with burglary is our own bias. The answer must also provide an understanding of Delaware County. This will make it easier to understand some of the activities burglars described in the interviews. It will allow better insight into the burglary process. We need to describe Delaware County not only as it is, but as a burgler might see it from his front doorstep.

Delaware County is a place like any other, literally. It is small in area, but contains one of the richest communities in America, one of the most deprived urban ghettos, pastoral farms, bedroom suburbs, tract homes and row homes. It is urban, rural and suburban. Some part of Delaware County probably shares a few attributes with almost every other area in America. This rich and varied socio-economic environment makes the county difficult for us to describe, but also presents a wide range of choices and opportunities for the burglar that recognizes them.

This "place like any other" is located in the southeast corner of Pennsylvania. It is bordered by the City of Philadelphia to the north and east, New Jersey across the Delaware River to the east, and the state of Delaware to the south. Areas to the west are predominantly rural. Delaware County is only 184.1 square miles. Its area ranks as the third smallest county in Pennsylvania, but it is the third most populous. Only Philadelphia and Allegheny Counties (Pittsburgh) have larger populations. Delaware County has 540,000 people according to the 1980 census. The population has declined from a 1970 high of 603,000. There are 50,000 black residents concentrated in Chester City and several municipalities close to Philadelphia. Principal among these are Darby Township and Yeadon Borough.

Delaware County is well ordered spatially. It is composed of three core areas. Each area is distinct and quite different from the others. The three areas are the Main Line, the bedroom suburbs, and the blue collar riverfront area. A brief description of each of these will give the reader a better feel for the county and the people who live there.

The Main Line

The northern portion of the county is a tier of towns and townships known as the Main Line. This area developed along Route 30, (better known as the Lancaster Pike) and the rail line that parallels the highway. The name Main Line is derived from the rail line that was built through the area in the 1800s. When it was built, the rail line was the most important east-west route of the Pennsylvania Railroad. It was truly the Main Line. It continues as a vital commuter rail link between this wealthy suburb and downtown Philadelphia. The area developed into a commuter suburb of great wealth because of the financial activities of Pennsylvania Railroad executives.

Prior to development of the Main Line, Philadelphia's wealthy lived in the center of the city or in a northern neighborhood called Chestnut Hill. The Pennsylvania Railroad financed the construction of the rail line by selling off the tracted land deeded to the railroad along the route. In order to maximize the profit gained through the sale, the railroad required its executives to settle on this land. This immediately turned the area into a prestigious place to live. These early ex-

ecutives were followed by other wealthy families eager to enjoy
country living within easy commuting distance to downtown
corporate jobs on the new rail line. The Main Line developed
into and remains one of the wealthiest and most prestigious
suburban areas in the United States. The Main Line is the
northern portion of Delaware County and continues into
Montgomery County to the north.

The Bedroom Suburbs

Just south of the Main Line begins the middle class bedroom suburbs of Philadelphia. The older sections of this area are boroughs. These are small towns with names like Darby, Sharon Hill, and Folcroft. Each has a small main street, an old business district, and a town hall. They blend one into another, making it difficult to tell where one town ends and another begins. Anyone not familiar with the area might have trouble telling the towns apart. The residential areas of these boroughs are tree lined streets with Victorian twin and row homes built of stone and brick. Streets of tightly packed row homes are nearest the business district. Apartment buildings are often found near main roads and train stations. These are old suburbs, built before World War II. They have small yards and aging sewer and water systems. Those closest to Philadelphia are beginning to experience many problems usually associated with urban areas, such as deterioration of the housing stock, falling property values and street crime. In broadest terms, these suburbs were built by and for a middle class made up of skilled workers and tradesmen, and they have developed little in the last 20 years.

The more recently developed bedroom suburbs are townships with names like Marple, Springfield and Nether Providence. Ranch, split level, colonial and Cape Cod style houses were built across large tracts of farm land to satisfy the post World War II housing demand. The communities closer to the city line generally have small lots and many twin homes. The trend to larger yards and homes continues farther west from Philadelphila. Average lots in Marple Township are one half acre, and, farther west in Concord township, the minimum size for new development is three acres.

These are the suburbs built to accommodate the baby boom, the expanding post war economy and white flight from the city. Their growth has been sustained by good schools and low taxes. The remaining land is being developed as townhouse condominiums, or expensive single family homes in rural settings. These areas were developed for a middle class of managers and white collar professionals. The term middle class is strained in townships like Concord and Birmingham. Home owners in these areas must have more than middle class resources to afford three acre parcels and $100,000 construction costs. For the most part, these bedroom communities continue to be white collar and middle class. They are stable areas where property values continue to appreciate.

The Blue Collar Riverfront

The third area is the blue collar region in the south and east portion of the county. The ribbon of land along the Delaware River has been the home of heavy industry for over 100 years. Baldwin Locomotive, Sun Shipyard, Westinghouse and Viscose were a few of the large companies to build plants in this area at the turn of the century. The Pennsylvania, the Reading and the B&O railroads all had major lines through this area. All of these industries were labor intensive. Soon this ribbon of land was a series of densely populated factory towns. The hub of this industry and commerce became the City of Chester.

Chester and the riverfront flourished in the first half of the 20th century. Immigrants from Italy, Poland and Ireland all found this a good place to work and raise a family. The rail lines, river, and proximity to major markets all made this an ideal location for industry. Heavy industry prospered, as did its blue collar workers.

Things began to change in the 1950s. The closing of Chester's Ford Motor Company auto plant in 1954 marked the beginning of a severe decline in the area. As the heavy smokestack industries closed or moved to the Sun Belt, a void was created in the social and economic life of the area. This void was not filled with other industries or businesses. Instead, the familiar pattern of unemployment, urban blight and poverty was set in motion.

Today this area of Delaware County remains a center of industry, but the prosperity is clearly gone. Boeing-Vertol, Sun Refining and Penn Ship still provide blue collar workers with jobs, but far fewer are at work these days (U.S. Bureau of

Census, 1973; 1983). Most of the blue collar communities on the riverfront have higher than average unemployment, lower mean incomes and older housing than the rest of the county or state. In spite of this there is a certain stability in places like Marcus Hook, Trainer and Eddystone. There is a feeling that the worst is over, and from this time on these communities will hold their own.

In the city of Chester, the decline brought on by the loss of industry was devastating, and the decline continues today. There is not a sense of stability about Chester, and there is little feeling within the community that things have hit bottom.

According to the United States Census reports, Chester City's population was over 66,000 in 1950. By 1980, the population had declined over 30 per cent to just 45,000. The population shifts were far more dramatic than the decrease implies because of the change in racial composition and employment. The number of blacks in Chester increased from 13,830 in 1950 to 26,009 in 1980. During this same thirty year period, the number of white residents declined from 52,174 to 19,076. Much of this change took place in the blue collar areas closest to the river. Unemployment and poverty continued to grow during this time. Chester's overall unemployment rate averaged 12.4 per cent in 1982, but in the most distressed part of the city, the rate is much higher. For nine of the city's nineteen census tracts that are the hardest hit, unemployment rates for 1982 ran between 13.5 and 66.7 per cent (Pennsylvania Department of Community Affairs, 1983). These are just a few of the social changes that accompanied the loss of industry.

Chester is just a shell of the vital center of commerce it once was, and the situation is not likely to improve. It is the least attractive area in the County to do business. Tax rates rise every year to make up for the loss in tax base as businesses continue to flee. Crime is endemic. The schools are rapidly deteriorating at a time when pervasive poverty offers the biggest challenge to the educational system. White flight left the downtown neighborhoods predominantly black, while the northern neighborhoods remained predominantly white, giving the city a segregated look. Chester is Delaware County's pocket of poverty.

The Diversity of Delaware County

Earlier we mentioned that suburban counties are an economic smorgasbord. Delaware County certainly qualifies. The transition from the poverty of Chester though blue collar and middle class suburbs provides a sharp contrast. The traditional wealth of the Main Line and the pastoral wealth of new developments in the western townships only widen the gap between rich and poor.

When we look at Delaware County we see diversity. This is illustrated in photographs that depict the progression of wealth and housing values from the poverty stricken south to the conspicuous wealth along the northern Main Line. For a burglar, this represents choices and decisions. We selected Delaware County because it was convenient and available. It turned out to be ideal.

Delaware County Prison

There is only one word to describe Delaware County Prison. The word is grim. It was constructed when local penal philosophy was one of punishment and confinement. It remains a very unpleasant place even in these more enlightened times. Its pastoral setting only adds to this austere building's isolation, rather than any sense of the freedom and openness of the green country that surrounds it. On our first visit to the prison, it seemed to rise from the horizon as we ascended a gentle country hillside road. It would not have been surprising had dark clouds gathered and lightening struck the center tower. The prison's grey and medieval demeanor dominates the surroundings, including the atmosphere inside.

The main entrance to the prison is double glass doors that open into a vestibule. The vestibule is marble and limestone

and always cool. It is an area that never seems bright enough. The cold appearance of the vestibule area is interrupted by the lights and logos of vending machines, and the heavy steel rolling bars that are the first step into the inside of the prison. Beyond the rolling bars is a control front desk area about eight feet wide and twelve feet long, with another set of equally imposing rolling bars just ahead. A prison guard operates the gate system from here, and supervises all movement in and out of the prison. The small, cramped area between the sets of rolling bars is the transitional area where visits are arranged, prisoners called from their cells, and all civilians sign in and out. Doors on either side of this small area lead to the offices of the warden and deputy warden. Waiting for prisoners to arrive for interviews, we often watched as criminals were brought in or taken away in handcuffs and shackles. Guards, staff, and visitors to the warden and deputy warden were always darting in and out of the doors on either side, leaving the impression that this closely controlled area was in chaos.

An interesting collection of people was always passing through the control area. Attorneys impatiently waited to visit their clients. The less experienced attorneys often offered complaints about the time required to escort a prisoner to the visiting area or the accommodations. There were also zealots of various descriptions waiting to talk to prisoners and help save them from demons like alcohol and narcotics, or teach them self sufficiency. Added to all this were the occasional probation and parole interviewers. They were very popular with the prisoners because their recommendations were often a direct route out.

Often we were forced to compete with a crew such as this for the limited space in the visiting area known as the "bull pen." The bull pen is the next area of the prison beyond the front desk. To reach it, we had to pass through the second set of heavy steel rolling bars. The mechanical grinding and final clank sound of these bars were further assurance that we were now farther inside than outside the prison.

The bull pen is long and narrow, perhaps ten feet wide. On either end of this area were small rooms partitioned off with plexiglass. Each room was supplied with a table and several chairs. It was only possible to hold a conversation in these rooms with the door closed to mute the din of activity outside. The central area between these two rooms was open and had only a few chairs. The entrance to the prison proper is a heavy steel door, controlled electronically from the front desk, that swings open and faces the second set of rolling bars. No two of these doors were ever open at one time. Only one set of rolling bars or the steel door are allowed open at any time. Each of our informants walked through this heavy steel door and into one of the side rooms for our interviews. The space for interviews and visits is obviously limited and closely controlled. Only three interviews or visits can go on at one time — less if one of the prisoners is considered a potential trouble maker. We soon learned that we could get one of the two partitioned rooms by arriving early, just a few minutes before the rest of the criminal justice community finished their first cup of coffee. Fortunately, this roughly coincided with the time when most prisoners were available and willing to accept visitors.

The idea of prisoners being available and willing seems curious considering their situation. It seemed almost too easy to just walk into the prison and ask to see someone. We later found that we had happened to pick the right time of day to conduct interviews. We arrived after breakfast and morning count up. Many prisoners would have been too busy to talk at another hour. There were a great number of activities going on inside, both optional and mandatory. Work, vocational training, high school courses, and counseling, all were ongoing each morning. Most prisoners who work, work in the prison kitchen. Our early arrival often found them just finished with work, but not yet occupied with another activity. Many prisoners enjoy and look forward to the wood shop or library. Many are actively pursuing their own legal defense, preparing each step, advising their lawyers or preparing their own petitions. Many prisoners have equipped their cells with televisions and stereos. And, we are sad to admit, some preferred the morning reruns or stereo tapes to the opportunity to talk about burglary with us. Much to our credit, our popularity rose after the first few interviews as word about us traveled through the prison.

Summary

What we were able to learn about the residential burglary process follows. We have divided it into three parts. The first is concerned with time and the opportunities and limits it places on both burglar and victim. How burglaries are fit into space, and the importance of perceptions of space in the burglary process form the second portion. The third section reviews some of the "nuts and bolts" techniques and reasons for their use described by the burglars. It also includes comments about suburban architecture, the burglary process, and suggestions about how the rising problem of residential burglary can be controlled.

CHAPTER II

THE USE OF TIME IN BURGLARY

Introduction

TIME IS A COMMODITY we take for granted. Our days are ordered and structured in such a way that we are seldom conscious of the passage of time. We only think about time when it marks a change in our behavior or activity. Work, class or television shows all cause us to consider time because we change what we are doing when these events begin and end. "It's time to go to class," or "lunch time" signal a temporal break in school or work activity. Daily time for most of us is actually highly structured and habitual (Pipkin, 1981). We give very little thought to time use in general, except of course when we are in a rush. We tend to take time for granted.

Professional burglars do not take time for granted. Time is a central concern to burglars for at least three reasons. First, they seek to minimize the time spent in locations that make their intent to burglarize obvious. This time is referred to in studies of burglary as "intrusion time." It also includes time spent on the outside of a premise forcing entry. Burglars try to keep this time as short as possible (Walsh, 1980, p, 89). Those who are good at their trade may spend no more than a minute or two forcing an entry and then only three to five minutes inside the house. This insures that they are no longer at the location when the authorities arrive, even if a silent alarm has signaled the police. Few suburban police departments can respond in less than three to five minutes, even if the alarm signal is transferred directly to the police car. Only amateur burglars will tarry at a crime scene long enough to be apprehended by a police person responding to a silent alarm.

Second, *opportunities* for burglary are time specific. The best opportunities occur only when target sites are unguarded. These times are predictable for suburban homes (Conklin and Bittner, 1973). Burglars have a certain folk wisdom about when these unguarded times occur during the day. We will discuss this in more detail later in this chapter.

Third, the time required to plan and execute a burglary has an effect on the potential non-criminal life of the burglar. The importance of this time is not only the length of its duration, but also the time of the day that it comes out of. The burglar must make himself available when the premises are least likely to be occupied. This requirement precludes other activities which start before, but continue through this time requirement. A legitimate job is a good example of this. It also precludes activities which would be done instead of, or at the same time as, the burglary.

Concepts About Time

These temporal components of the burglary process will form the basis of this chapter. Before we discuss each in detail, some conceptual background is needed. This background is taken from research completed by Swedish geographers, particularly Thorsten Hagerstrand (Hagerstrand, 1970, 1975; Carlstein, Parkes and Thrift, 1978). Their work suggests that our daily activities have a profound effect on what is possible and impossible for us to do, simply because of the time these activities require. Certain activities must be undertaken. These are termed non-discretionary activities. Other activities are done by choice. These are called discretionary activities. Each person's day can be separated into times which are non-discretionary and those that are discretionary (Chapin, 1978). As we shall see, the non-discretionary times provide the most important opportunities for burglary.

Each unit of discretionary and non-discretionary time extends until it is interrupted by another non-discretionary activity—something you must do. These units of time are termed time blocks. The temporal extent of each block is as important as the frequency with which they occur. This is how our non-discretionary daily activities tend to structure our time. Many discretionary activities require a certain amount of time. If this amount of time is not available before a non-discretionary activity must be performed, the individual is effectively precluded from this activity. You can't go to see a two-hour movie on your lunch hour and still return to work on time. There are also occasions when non-discretionary activities, which are brief but frequent, preclude many uses of the discretionary time in between. The lot of the housewife is a good example.

Time Blocks of Victims

Women have been the guardians of the home throughout history (Loyd, Monk and Rengert, 1982; Miller, 1982). Men usually work outside the home, leaving the family in the care of women who work in or near the home. Although this traditional pattern is changing somewhat (with women spending less time within the home), it has not reversed (Mazey and Lee, 1983). It is unusual to find a man working in the home while the woman works outside the home. If the home is guarded during the workday, it is guarded by a woman in most cases. If it is not guarded by a woman, it is likely to be unguarded. The use of time by women in our society is, therefore, more central to the issue of residential burglary than the use of time by men.

In traditional American society, women have shorter blocks of discretionary time available to them than men (Palm and Pred, 1974). Men work for large blocks of time and then are relatively free for large blocks of time. Women have these large blocks of time punctuated by family responsibilities. A housewife's day, as mentioned, has a considerable amount of discretionary time that can't effectively be put to use because of the frequent occurrence of brief, non-discretionary household chores. Taking children to school takes little time, but rules out most activities prior to the trip. It also rules out many activities that begin before the trip, but last long into the day, when the housewife may have a great deal of discretionary time. Several brief non-discretionary activities can totally structure a long block of time. Recognition of this problem is evident in the extended hours of supermarkets, the marketing of educational programs at a variety of hours, and flex time in the work place. Although this pattern is changing rapidly for some in contemporary American society, many women are still precluded from certain activities by the length of time required to accomplish them.

Consider a hypothetical and in some ways typical housewife. She awakens at about 6:15 a.m. on weekdays and begins her morning work. This is nondiscretionary time and she has little alternative to these activities. (We assume that she receives little or no help from the other members of the family.) At 7:30, she may drive children to school or her husband to the train station for his commute to work. By 9 or 10 a.m., her non-discretionary obligatons are just about over and she has one and a half to three hours of time to do what she likes — discretionary time. This time may be used to visit friends, read, or watch television.

Whatever her choice may be, she tends to do the same thing most days. Leisure time activities are habit forming. Sometime around mid day she prepares and eats lunch. After lunch, our hypothetical housewife again has a block of discretionary time. Her obligation to household chores reappears about 2 or 2:30 p.m. when she must prepare for her family to arrive home. At 3:30 she may begin picking up children and her husband. Non-discretionary duties focused on the evening meal take up the time from 3:30 until about 7 p.m. Finally, she is free to spend time with her family or as she chooses from about 7:30 until bed time.

Note that except for the last block of discretionary time, all of the blocks of free time available to the housewife occur in short spans. These short periods of time are also scattered throughout the day. This precludes her from performing any task, discretionary or non-discretionary, that might require more than an hour or two during the daytime.

From the perspective of a potential burglar, there are few times when this person's home is unguarded. These times are outlined on the accompanying graph. Predictable non-discretionary times may be identified as the times the house-wife drives her husband to the commuter train station or the children to school each day. She may repeat the task to bring the family home again in the late afternoon. These tasks provide plenty of time for a residential burglary. Predictable events in time provide a perceptive burglar with many potential opportunities.

Discretionary times spent outside the home are predictable when housewives fall into temporal habits concerning shopping or visiting friends and relatives. These times are generally right after the children leave for school in the morning, or in the early afternoon right after lunch. Many women do their daily shopping at the same time every day. These habitual discretionary activities can also be observed and predicted by res-

HOME GUARDIANSHIP OF NONEMPLOYED AND EMPLOYED WOMEN

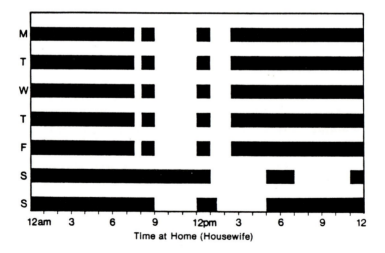

Time at Home (Housewife)

idential burglars. These discretionary times are different because they can be altered. If a housewife lives in a high crime area, she can plan some random behavior into her otherwise structured day to break the routine.

Weekends are different from weekdays. Saturday afternoons are likely to be spent at a shopping mall. Saturday nights might be spent visiting friends or at a movie or concert. Sunday mornings traditionally are given over to church, although many choose to sleep late. Typical Sunday afternoon activities might include visiting friends or a trip to the park, and Sunday nights are generally spent at home. For many, the weekend ends with an early bedtime Sunday night in anticipation of Monday morning's return to work. While the specifics may vary, these examples illustrate the many opportunities predictable time use creates for a burglary.

The example of the hypothetical housewife is deliberately simple and traditional. In reality, her day probably is much more cluttered with mundane activities that are non-discretonary, but not reoccurring. For example, if the hypothetical housewife's day were to be further complicated by doctor or veterinary appointments, caring for an elderly parent, or any of the infinite number of things people must do in the course of a day, the time available to her would be reduced further. It should not be surprising that an increasing number of women are choosing not to become full time housewives. They desire to work and do other activities that are not possible given the small blocks of time available to traditional housewives.

The case of the woman working outside the home is quite different. She may perform many of the same tasks as women who work only in the home until 8 or 8:30 a.m. At this time, she may leave the home for a distant work place until at least noon. Some women who work outside the home return home for lunch. Then they are back at work from one o'clock until four or five in the afternoon. They are likely to return home around this time, and their day again proceeds along the lines of the woman who does not work outside the home. Notice that the only time this woman may be home is around lunch

Time at Home (Employed Woman)

time. This is a short time block, less than one hour, when the house is guarded. The rest of the work day, the home is likely to be unguarded and susceptible to burglary.

Weekends of working women often start after the evening meal on Friday. Unfortunately, a lot of the weekend is devoted to the chores that are usually performed during the week. Saturday morning is spent on housework or the laundry. Saturday afternoon may be used for shopping and Saturday night for entertainment. Sunday morning at ten thirty or eleven may be spent at a late church service, while Sunday afternoon may be spent at a park. Many Sunday mornings or afternoons may also be spent at the supermarket food shopping. Sunday nights are spent at home, often preparing for Monday morning work. From the graph, it is easy to identify times when these hypothetical houses are unguarded.

When we combine the daily activities of many women, we can identify times when typical houses are not likely to be guarded. There are few studies that have examined the time use of many women combined (Chapin, 1974). The most extensive study to our knowledge is a study of British women conducted by the British Broadcasting Corporation to plan daytime programming (Shapcott and Steadmann, 1978). This study is important because it examines the reasons people did not watch television, as well as simply when they did not watch. The most important reason for not watching television is being away from home and engaged in some other non-discretionary activity. Two graphs taken from this study illustrate when British women are most likely not to be home by hour of the day.

The times women who work outside the home are most likely to be found at home are illustrated in the first graph. These times are at noon and late afternoon. Burglars tend to avoid these times in practice, along with weeknights and early morning hours.

The second graph is for women who do not work outside the home. Their houses are most likely to be unoccupied in the late morning (10 to 11 o'clock) and in the early afternoon (1 to 3 o'clock). It is not surprising that these are the preferred times for burglars to work in the United States (Reppetto, 1974; Scarr, 1973). The burglars we interviewed preferred to work at certain times of the day. These times are also illustrated on this graph. Here we expect burglaries to be high when the proportion of women working in the home is low. Notice that their burglary patterns follow more closely the habits of women working outside the home than those who do not. The afternoon increase in burglary is the only time that corresponds well with women not likely to be home who also work within the home. Most of the nighttime burglars we interviewed operated on weekend nights. Again, there is a close correspondence with the times houses are likely to be unguarded on weekends.

By comparing these two graphs, we see that women are least likely to be home in the late morning and early afternoon hours. This holds true for both women who work outside the home and those who do not. This makes the time blocks from nine to eleven a.m. and one to three p.m. likely times to find homes unoccupied. The comings and goings of members of traditional households do not go unnoticed by burglars. The

HOME GUARDIANSHIP AND RESIDENTIAL BURGLARY

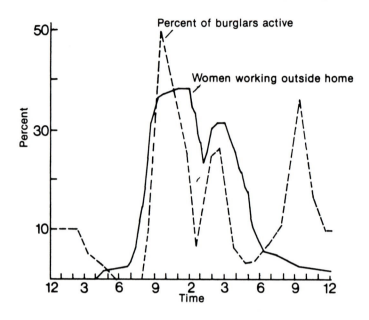

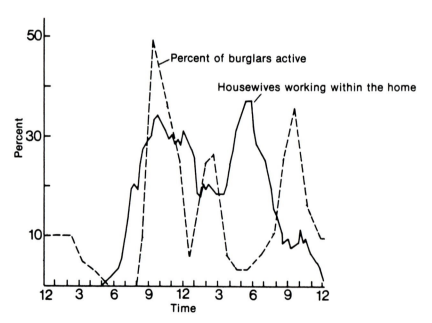

burglars we talked to had a clear perception of how families use time and when homes were most likely unguarded. Their perception is clearer than the average citizen because of the high risks involved in their criminal occupation.

Time and the Process of Burglary

This returns us to the burglary process and the question of how burglars find empty homes to burglarize. The burglars we talked to each had their own perception about time use and opportunity. We asked what time they liked to commit burglaries and why. Their answers are diverse, and sometimes tell us as much about the burglar as his victim.

One burglar who specialized in homes in prestigious neighborhoods such as Bala Cynwyd and Penn Wynn clearly understood Main Line social behavior. "On Friday nights and Saturday nights, most people go out to dinner or to concerts, whatever. If they're not home watchin' TV, and you can always tell if they're watchin' TV because of the glow, then they're gone for the night." A different, but equally perceptive approach was, "Just drive around in the area between, maybe 7:30 and 8:30 in the morning, and just look for folks goin' out. If it's a man and his wife dressed for work — you know they're gone at least for the morning." Another less sophisticated comment was, "Women generally go shopping at one or two o'clock in the afternoon. That's the best time to find no one at home."

The point, of course, is always to find times when homes would be empty with some certainty. The burglars used their intuitive knowledge of time blocks to predict the occurrence of discretionary or non-discretionary activities that would offer a safe house and enough time to burglarize it. This intuition was always confirmed by observation. Casing the house, watching it carefully, is usually followed by a direct walk to the front door to "Ring the bell about a hundred times or so." One burglar would read the name on the mailbox, go to a phone, look up the number and call the house. He knew the house was probably empty if there was no answer.

Other answers were similar to these. Interestingly, few of

the professional burglars liked to operate late at night. The only exceptions were those who were under the influence of hallucinogens such as LSD. The reason late night burglaries were unpopular was simply because it was too difficult to tell if anyone was home. As several burglars put it, "That's the way you get yourself shot." The burglars were afraid of sound sleepers who wouldn't respond to the doorbell but might awaken once they had entered the house. Most burglars go to great lengths to avoid this sort of confrontation (Walsh, 1980). This includes careful consideration of their own ideas and notions about traditional time blocks. Burglars use their ideas about time to try to predict when homes are most likely to be vacant. Burglars are very alert to clues about when someone is at home. They use every possible indication to succeed, including their knowledge of traditional time blocks.

Crime prevention specialists warn against "signals" that alert burglars that no one is home (Galub, 1970; Burns, 1967; Furlong, 1968). Uncollected mail and newspapers in the driveway are examples. Burglars also notice subtle things like closed windows and air conditioners that are not on during very hot days. Some people pull all their window shades down as they leave home to keep people from seeing inside. Few of us would live in a house with all the shades pulled down all day. The objective should be to make a house look lived in, not empty. We should never signal outsiders that the house is empty. For many burglars these signals are open invitations.

The whole concept of time use will require a thorough and rigorous examination before we are able to understand and predict the impact of time use on criminal activity. For example, further insight is needed in areas such as the impact that changing life styles may have on the times when homes are unoccupied and vulnerable (Cohen and Felson, 1979). A related issue is the appropriateness of suburban architectural styles. Built for a traditional household with women at home much of the day, most suburban houses are ill suited to the contemporary two career household. The architectural design of recently constructed homes in urban areas undergoing "gentrification" offers an interesting comparison.

Residents moving to areas undergoing gentrification in central cities can generally be characterized as young, professional and upper middle class. Most marriages include two careers. The comparison in house style reveals differences that reflect not so much the differing crime rate of the two areas, as the contrasting life styles of the inhabitants. One thing is clear: large picture windows and sliding glass doors in secluded suburban homes that are unoccupied for long periods of time during the day may no longer be appropriate. We will discuss this in more detail in a later section.

This raises a question abut the extent to which the higher rate of crime in the inner city may be due to the fact that many urban homes are unguarded during much of the day in single person and two-career households. We ought to consider how much of the currently escalating suburban residential burglary rate may be due to the increasing opportunity afforded by homes unoccupied during the work day. More and more homes are left unoccupied as women enter the work force in larger numbers (Cohen and Felson, 1978). It is clear to us that many of the burglars we interviewed contributed to the local increase in residential burglary rates because of their intuitive understanding of time use. We know so little about the issue of "home guardianship" or how to render our homes safe. This is especially important in two-career households.

Time Blocks of Criminals

This brings us to the other side of the issue. If late morning and early afternoon are the best times for committing residential burglaries, what effect does this have on the discretionary and non-discretionary time blocks of residential burglars? That is, what effect does this have on their lives? In this section, we will illustrate that the time block required for burglary has a profound effect on the lives of burglars. In fact, it may require rethinking many of the contemporary views concerning rehabilitation of property criminals; more about rehabilitation later.

How much time is required to commit a residential burglary? One of the authors asked this queston in several academic meetings as well as in several criminology classes. The answer invariably was, "Somewhere around three to five minutes." This time block should not affect anyone's life. It could be accommodated over a coffee break or on the way to work. A burglar could fit it in almost anywhere during his or her day. In fact, these people were considering only "intrusion time" when they answered "three to five minutes." This is only the time the residential burglar is actually in the house. Professional burglars try to minimize this time as much as possible.

What they did not consider is the time required to complete the other aspects of a residential burglary — the time that a professional burglar often trys to maximize to a limit. For example, a professional residential burglar will spend considerable time casing the house and making sure no one is at home. These tasks are best performed slowly and carefully. Only at the point of forced entry does the burglar become acutely aware of time used as a critical element. From the point of forced entry forward, the burglar races to minimize the time until the stolen goods are out of his possession and replaced by cash from a fence.

Our data from Delaware County indicate that the median
time required to commit a residential burglary when a car is
used is over two hours. This includes the time from the moment the burglar leaves home until he returns (or has fenced
the goods). This does not include what we call "prep time."
Prep time is the time used to plan the burglary. For some, it is
used for drinking or using narcotics to get in the correct frame
of mind, or gathering together tools and/or accomplices. In
any case, the time involved can be significant. It ranged from
six hours for a residential burglar who burglarized several
houses a day, to fifteen minutes for a "smash and grab" burglar
who broke windows and took valuables from the window sill or
porch and left.

Let's turn our attention to how burglars fit this time requirement into their daily lives. We found that it had a dramatic effect on the lives of almost all the burglars. Some
examples will illustrate this point. One example is chosen from
each of the major time blocks of the day: morning; afternoon;
and night. The data were collected by asking each burglar to
trace through a typical day from the time they woke up in the
morning until they went to bed at night. This was done for
both a typical week day and a typical weekend day. This provided us with a time diary of typical days for these individuals.
Then, we asked each to fit their burglary activities into these
days (if they had not already indicated it), and how long it took
for each component of the burglary. That is, how much time
and at what time of the day did the burglar search for a house,
case it, break in, and return home.

The subjects genuinely enjoyed thinking back to their lives
outside the prison. They had little trouble describing typical
days. This is consistent with expectations since most humans
tend to develop habitual patterns of daily time use. We tend to
get up at certain times, perform certain tasks (some of which
are non-discretionary) at certain times and end our days at
certain times. Most of us could also easily construct a diary of
a typical day in our past.

For example, many people have their alarm set for a specific time to awaken each morning. They eat breakfast at a certain time and leave for work at a set time. They return from work at a certain time and then eat dinner at the same time each day. Then, a more or less set routine is followed until bedtime. Our burglars remembered and described for us their own structured days. The examination of the diaries of a few of the burglars we interviewed will illustrate this.

How burglar #26 ordered his day and the distance he traveled from his home to carry out each activity of the day is shown in the accompanying illustration. The time of day in hours appears along the left side of the graph. The distance he traveled during these time blocks to carry out his burglary activity on a typical day appear on the bottom of the graph.

Follow the graph as we trace through a typical day of criminal activity with the burglar. Burglar #26 is a good example of a mid-morning burglar. He would sleep until 8:30 a.m., wake up, eat, and leave home at about 9:30. This individual lived in a middle class community and did not need to drive far to locate what he considered "good houses" to burglarize. He said he just "drove for five minutes or so down the main highway," and then turned into a residential community that he "felt" might be good. He would spend 30 minutes to one hour looking for just the right house. He would spend another 30 minutes casing it to be certain no one was home and that there was no unexpected activity nearby. He would then break in, burglarize the house, fence the goods and be home by noon. The total time required for this individual to commit a typical burglary was two and a half hours. This constituted his "crime time." It used up all his morning hours.

Burglar #26 worked, but he quit his job because he used heroin, and burglary was the only way he could pay for his drug habit. He had to quit his job to commit morning burglaries because the time blocks required for each conflicted. When he worked, he drove a taxi cab. He used the following time blocks when working. He woke up at 6:30 a.m. and left home at 7:00 to catch the morning rush hour business. He drove the cab all day until 6:00 at night; ate dinner and watched television until 11:00, and then went to sleep. His

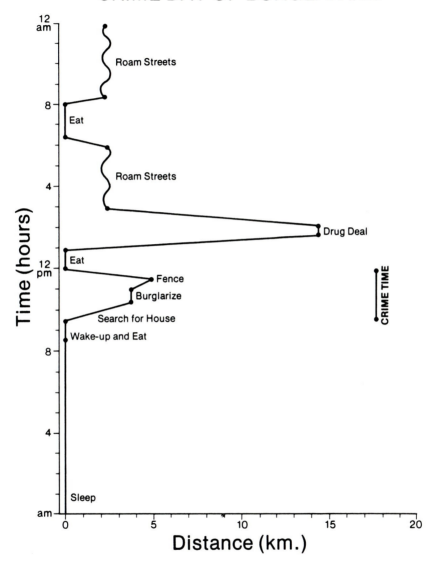

CRIME DAY OF BURGLAR #26

criminal time blocks came out of his mid-morning worktime. He chose a life of crime to support his drug habit. He could not work and burglarize during the same blocks.

Individual #28 is an afternoon burglar. He worked while active as a burglar. He simply called in sick toward the end of the week and took a day off for crime. He was not a drug user, although he acquired an addiction to gambling in Atlantic City casinos. (As an aside, his descriptions of his forays to Atlantic City left us both a little envious. Recent published accounts of bank embezzler Bryan Malony illustrates both the addiction to gambling and the amount of money that can be used to support this addiction (Bissinger, 1984).) Individual #28 reasoned that the only means of collecting enough money to gamble over a weekend was to burglarize at least one day a week. This day was during the latter part of the week, usually a Thursday afternoon.

Trace through a typical crime day for burglar #28 on the graph. During a burglary day, individual #28 would call in sick at 8:30 in the morning and go back to sleep. He would wake up at noon, eat, and leave the house by 1:00. His method of operation was somewhat more complex than other burglars, and it required a little more time. After he found a likely house to burglarize, he would spend 30 minutes to case it. Then he would drive his car around to the area immediately behind the house. He would open his trunk and remove a "dirt bike," a small motorcycle built to run over unpaved areas. He would ride his bike to the victim's street and park it three or four houses away. He reasoned that if anything went wrong, he could ride the dirt bike across the expansive yards and woods of this suburban area. On the dirt bike, he could easily outdistance anyone chasing him by foot or auto. He could always retrieve his car later. This technique added about 30 minutes to his "crime time" and he did not return home until about 4:00 p.m. The total time required for this crime block was three hours.

This individual could meet a work schedule and commit burglaries because he restricted himself to one or two burglary days a week. His job was janitorial work for a house and office

CRIME DAY OF BURGLAR #28

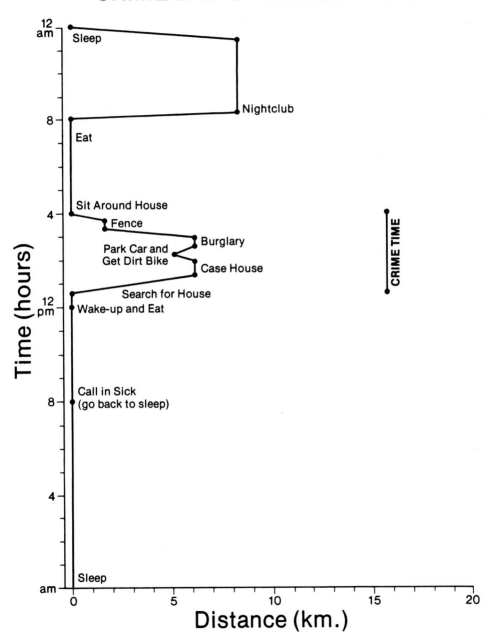

cleaning firm. Individual #28 reasoned that the firm was accustomed to high job turnover and frequent no shows because
of the relatively low pay scale and menial tasks. He was not
sure how much longer the frequency of his sick days would be
tolerated. He felt that sooner or later they would catch on to
his regular pattern of absences and either force him to work
more regularly or fire him. If that time of reckoning ever arrived, individual #28 had no doubt about the course he would
follow. As he stated, "I could make more burglarizing in one
day than for a week's work as a janitor." Traditional employment could not compete with crime economically or socially.
Burglary paid better and was a lot more fun than janitorial
work.

He was apprehended for burglary before he was faced with
this choice. The way he was caught illustrates what can go
wrong in a burglar's life even when extreme care is taken.
Keep in mind that he was an early afternoon burglar.

The day he was apprehended he had followed all his usual
precautions to the letter. He had cased the house for a long
time and found no activity in the area. He rode his dirt bike
around and walked slowly toward the house, observing the
area carefully again. He then approached the house and rang
the door bell "twenty times." There was no answer. He "jimmied a window" and climbed inside. He unlocked the front
and back doors to provide alternate escape routes, a sign of a
proficient burglar. Then he proceeded to the master bedroom,
removed a pillow case and started to fill it with jewelry and
money from the dresser tops and drawers. He worked quickly
and moved from the master bedroom directly to the dining
room. There he gathered the best of the silver serving dishes
and utensils.

What he didn't realize during this efficient routine was that
a daughter of the family was lying in an upstairs bedroom, sick
with the flu. Although she would normally be in school, the flu
had kept her at home. She was sick enough that she did not
answer the door. But she was strong enough to pick up the
phone and call her brother when she heard someone break into
the house. Her brother was only several blocks away. The

burglar was on his way out the back door, and unaware of all this, when he encountered the brother running toward the house.

At this point, his escape plan went into action. He headed toward his dirt bike at a dead run but realized he would not be able to get it started before the brother would reach him. He veered off and started running in a large circle to put some distance between them. Our burglar tried a final ploy that he indicated "always works." He reached down and grasped the bottom of the pillow case and flung the contents into the middle of the street. As he put it, "Nine out of ten people will stop and try to gather up their silver and stuff. But this guy didn't miss a stride. He kept coming. So I gave up and we went back and picked everything up together."

Even the best laid plans sometimes go wrong. The time of day was right for no one to be home — but someone was. If you ring a doorbell twenty times, even someone engrossed in a television show will become irritated enough to answer — but not a teenage girl home alone with the flu. Even if someone does hear you break in, you will be out and gone before they can respond unless a relative or the police are nearby. The odds are strongly in favor of the burglar, but sometimes everything goes wrong. That's usually how a good burglar is caught, through a run of bad luck that is far from common.

Burglar #23 liked early evening on Saturday nights. He had a target demand of $2,000 that he tried to hit every burglary night. He would keep burglarizing houses until he felt he had this amount in fenceable goods even if it took him until one o'clock Sunday morning. He also is a good example of an individual who required "prep time" before he started out. He liked to smoke marijuana because he felt it "increased my sense of hearing." Under the influence of "pot," he felt he could hear people breathing if they were at home. He also felt he could hear someone coming home long before they entered the house, allowing him plenty of time to escape. The total time required for #23's night of burglary was generally three to four hours.

Since he only burglarized on Saturday nights, his criminal

CRIME DAY OF BURGLAR #23

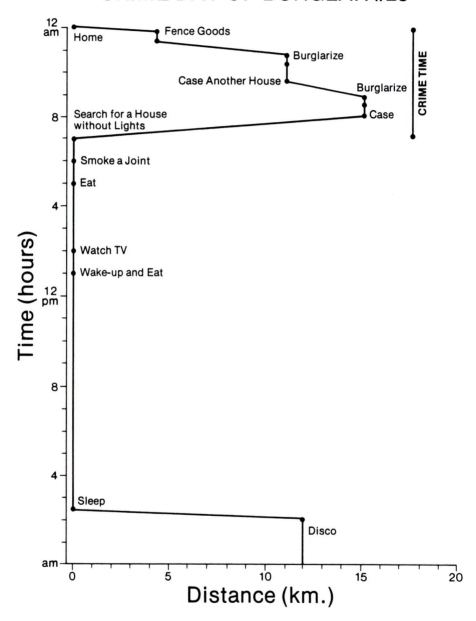

activity time cut only into his discretionary "bar time." He could work week days as a store clerk although he was often tired at work. He also frequently called in sick. However, as long as he continued his Saturday night modus operandi, his job and criminal activity did not conflict. He was unusual in this manner from most of the other individuals we interviewed.

For example, individual #31 is an individual who was a computer programmer for a large utility company in downtown Philadelphia. He was introduced to heroin while serving in Viet Nam. After the war, he entered a treatment program at a methadone clinic. While working as a programmer, he stopped at the methadone clinic at the Veteran's Hospital in Philadelphia on his way to work. Gradually though, he went back to heroin and found that the only way he could support his habit was through crime. Although he was a highly paid computer programmer, he could make much more at full time burglary, so he quit his job for crime. He couldn't both work and commit burglaries because the times he chose for burglary conflicted with the hours he was scheduled to work.

Another burglar we interviewed, #34, refused to let his job as a wall board installer get in the way of his career as a burglar. He was active in late 1980 when the price of gold was rising rapidly. He quit his job to devote all his time to burglary, as well as spending his considerable income. When asked if he commited more than one burglary a day he responded, "When the price of gold broke $600 an ounce, I did three or four a day sometimes."

Working is incompatible with crime for many. And many individuals like #34 quit good jobs to make more money at crime — money especially needed for drugs or gambling. The point is that many criminals are unemployed at the time they are arrested. And this fact is well documented in many survey interviews and official statistics (Gibbs and Shelly, 1982; Letkemann, 1973). What is *not* detected is what caused the unemployment. In many cases, unemployment is not what caused crime. Crime caused the unemployment. Time conflicts forced individuals to choose burglary or their jobs. The

WORKING DAY OF BURGLAR #31

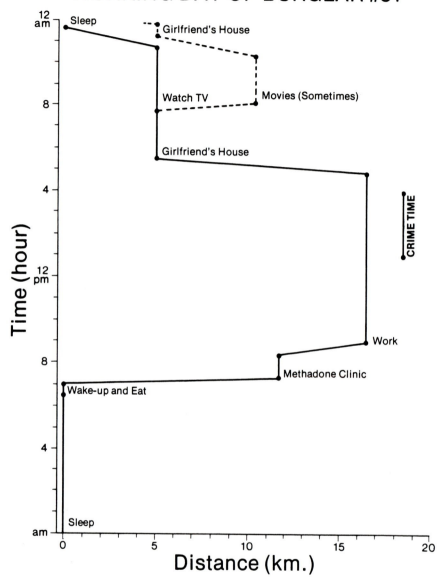

resolution of the conflict led directly to unemployment.

Reppetto (1974, p. 73) noted the choice between work and crime in his study of burglars in Boston. "In a sense, the choice of a criminal career appears logical for many of the interviewees, given their consumption preferences and the legitimate options open to them to satisfy those preferences. Burglary, after all, did appear to offer a relatively good return for independent work and little tedium — vocational benefits hard to attain for the relatively unskilled and uneducated." He also notes that only seven percent of the interviewed burglars had *never* been employed (Reppetto, 1974, p. 102). This same theme is the topic of Plate's *Crime Pays* (Plate, 1975).

Researchers need to probe a little deeper to ascertain whether crime is the "chicken or the egg." It would not surprise us if crime caused more unemployment than unemployment caused crime in suburban areas. However, this relationship may be reversed in the inner city. At this point, our findings are only suggestions. It will require further corroboration to establish the relationship. Yet the evidence is strong enough in this study to suggest that policy advisors in the criminal justice community reevaluate the wisdom of traditional assumptions concerning crime and employment.

Employment and Rehabilitation

We have already mentioned that unemployment for some burglars is a result of their choice of crime over a legitimate job as a way to earn money. This choice is forced on some burglars by the financial demand of individual psychology or physiological needs. Few jobs pay well enough to support a drug or gambling addiction. Many prison programs mistake the symptoms for the disease. Programs that train individuals in metal work, mechanics, carpentry or other craft skills miss completely the root cause of the crime. The financial demands of addiction lead to unemployment and crime. Rehabilitation in the form of job training is not likely to end the burglary career of a heroin addict unless it is matched with a far more powerful addiction treatment program.

Some individuals turn to burglary because it is more challenging, interesting, and lucrative than the workaday world. Burglars we interviewed often left what they felt were menial or boring jobs to devote their time to crime because they "liked the way it feels." The planning process and the danger involved provided them with something missing in their jobs as laborers. Burglary is not as physically demanding and pays better. A burglar interviewed by Reppetto (1974) stated, "I don't like to work. I haven't had to work for five years. You can make a week's pay in one night." One individual we interviewed combined his job and burglary activities. While working as a roofer, #12 would case houses surrounding the home being roofed. He observed the activities of a household, and noted the patterns of time use over several days. After the roofing crew moved to another location he would return to the area and use the information he gathered on the job to execute a successful burglary. What are the rehabilitation possibilities for people who use their jobs or leave them in favor of a career in burglary? Will training in carpentry deter a person who has already chosen burglary to supplement a career in roofing?

The process of integrating property criminals back into everyday life cannot begin until their individual psychological and medical needs have been treated. Only after changes in their psychological and physiological needs have been achieved will programs in job training and other practical life skills have a chance of success.

Gambling or drug addiction treatment programs are aimed at changing the physiological and psychological needs of the individual. Going beyond this basic approach is a program of intensive parole to restructure the daily habits and routines of the individual (Gettinger, 1983). The goal of this program is to restructure the daily habits of the individual to conform to those of law abiding society. This approach acknowledges that individuals cannot divorce their actions (however trivial they may seem) from the total workings of society. All of our actions, as well as our inaction, are part of the sum total of the society we live in. Our actions and activities will either benefit our society as a whole, or society must absorb and suffer the negative impact of what we each do.

These thoughts are summarized well by Pred (1981, p. 246) when he writes about the effects of time use on society. "There is nothing that can affect the time geography or path of an individual without affecting the time-geographic workings of society as a whole, nor is there anything that can affect the time-geographic workings of society without affecting the path of an individual. Any time a person freely or involuntarily commits a segment of her daily path and finite time resources to an activity bundle of an institutional or organizatonal project, she subtracts from the total daily time resources of society as a whole in a given area. She thereby reduces the number of other institutional or organizational project-activity bundles that can be packed into the time-space organization of that same, already defined portion of society."

In other words, the time use of an individual is a zero sum game with respect to society. Every time we commit time to one activity, we take that time away from other potential activities. We can only do one thing at a time, in one place at a time. Our goal should be to encourage time use that will be beneficial to society, and discourage time uses that are a detriment to society as a whole.

How can these ideas be put to work? Time use that is beneficial can become habit forming, through repetition or training (Pipkin, 1981). It can become a way of life. There are promising programs in several states that incorporate these principals in probation and parole programs (Gettinger, 1983).

The "intensive probation supervision" program used in Georgia is the most promising. Unlike previous attempts at intensive supervision, this program does not simply rely on more frequent than usual "check ups" by the probation officer. Instead, the probation officer attempts to restructure the time use of each probationer's life. First, there is a curfew. No probationer can spend discretionary night time outside their home. This eliminates the possibility of night time crime outside the home. During the day, probationers must hold a job and engage in voluntary community service programs. Probationers must earn enough to pay a monthly fee to help defray the cost of the intensive supervision. These activities tie up much of the probationers' discretionary time during daylight hours. The time that remains is in small blocks scattered throughout the day. Some of this time must be used for meals and personal care. There is little idle time to plan and execute crimes. This is especially true of residential burglaries that are best performed in the middle of the work day when most people are not home.

Employment is at the heart of the Georgia program. If a probationer loses his job, he or she must actively search for another. If the habits formed during this intensive supervision period are permanent, probation may actually succeed in doing what it is designed to accomplish.

There is a test underway in California to see if this type of intensive supervision can change the lives of juvenile delinquents (Wiederanders, 1983). In Delaware, Governor du Pont has proposed a ten level sanction system. The core of the program is employment and intensive supervision (du Pont, 1984). Programs that actively attempt to restructure the time use of offenders around gainful employment have great promise for success.

A strong suggestion made by these observations is that employment and job continuity are key behavioral indicators of successful probation. Finding and keeping a job are good indicators that a probationer has adjusted to life outside prison. Frequent absenteeism, loss of a job, or quitting outright are likely signs that the probationer is not performing up to society's standards.

Traditional parole officers with caseloads of one hundred or more cannot provide the degree of supervision required to track the daily activities of early probationers and parolees. Intensive parole assigns no more than thirty cases to each officer (Gettinger, 1983). Curfews can then be set and enforced. Many other activities in the new lives being established must be monitored as well. Releasing prisoners with little or no initial supervision can achieve nothing but failure and result in high recidivism rates.

Job training should be part of any prison experience. The

job training should be for jobs that are more than menial, and that the prisoner will have some chance of finding in the outside world. Jobs should be actively sought or provided at the time prisoners are paroled. This has always been the most difficult part of parole. If jobs are secured, we suggest as a condition of parole that jobs be successfully held. A parole officer should be aware of potential problems if a job is terminated by a parolee without good cause. A poor work record and frequent absenteeism might be an even earlier warning. These are indications that the parolee has not adjusted to society and has chosen a different use for his time other than work. How the parolee's time is being put to use should be cause for concern.

It should be very clear now that for many in our society crime pays. And sometimes, it pays very well. Crime is necessary for most that choose to use drugs or gamble heavily (Inciardi, 1979; Bissinger, 1984). It is also very profitable for some who just want to live comfortably (Jackson, 1969; Jeffery, 1968). Consider the odds associated with each step of the criminal justice process that must be taken before a burglar is sentenced to prison. Prison, rather than arrest, is the burglar's worst fear.

The chances of being removed from society for any specific burglary in the Philadelphia region are approximately the same as for contracting polio. For example, many burglaries are never reported to the police, and of those reported only a small fraction (maybe less than 5%) lead to an apprehension (Conklin and Bittner, 1973). Only a few of those caught are charged and brought to trial. Finally, at long last, some of those brought to trial are found guilty. Only six in one thousand convicted burglars in the metropolitan Philadelphia area are sentenced to prison (Epstein, 1978). It is common knowledge on the street that hardly anything ever happens to most burglars. Only a long streak of bad luck leads to prison.

The probability increases little for repeat offenders. What are the risks? How long can a burglar operate before being caught? Once apprehended, there is the labyrinth court process that often leads to dismissal of charges or verdicts of not guilty. Those tried and convicted do not face much of a penalty. As noted by Reppetto (1974, p. 24), "The typical older offender has been breaking and entering for many years, and has been in and out of jail several times on many different charges."

The message for the street wise is, "The first one is on the house." Often, the first offense carries no real punishment or hope of correction. Much of this is the result of full prisons, crowded with individuals convicted of far more brutal crimes, and the overwhelming caseload of probation and parole officers. There is little room left for burglars. There is a public perception of this condition. It is demonstrated in the way criminal acts are discounted as a way of life (Letkemann, 1973). Clearly, prison is not the answer for criminals who hold any hope of rehabilitation. Prisons often teach techniques of crime better than techniques of survival in law abiding society. Intensive supervision outside of jail holds much more promise of altering the lives of those who are leaning toward a life of crime.

The published results of a study by Ball, Rosen, Flueck and Nurco (1981) are our best glimpse at the true relationship between drug abuse and crime. Their study demonstrates that many heroin addicts commit crimes almost every day of their addicted lives. Every burglar we interviewed who had been a drug addict confirmed this finding. Crime becomes part of the addict's mundane routine. It becomes part of his daily life. Crime is of little concern to the addict beyond when it can be fit into his day; and around his constant need.

Drug abuse provides a useful example of our failures to understand burglary as the result of a decision. We need to spend more of our efforts determining what leads to these decisions and what we can do to change them. Drug abuse has always been treated symptomatically at best. Our attention is too often directed to the attributes associated with crime that are difficult, if not impossible to change. Our efforts would be better spent on issues we can more easily identify, and, we hope, change. The use of time in our society is one such issue. Useful, productive habits of time use can be taught.

Comments and Conclusions

The awareness and use of time blocks by residential burglars is remarkable. This section began by pointing out that most of us take time for granted. Clearly, burglars do not. Residential burglars think about when and why a person is not likely to be at home and they use these ideas in their burglary activity.

One burglar, for example, unraveled an extremely successful way to predict both a safe time block and a financially successful venture. He researched a Philadelphia professional sports team and learned the home addresses of most of its players. During home games when wives were almost certain to be at the games, he would burglarize the home of a team member. Often, he would listen to the game while inside the house. The affluent athletes always seemed to have expensive jewelry and cash on hand making these burglaries very lucrative. This burglar was so confident about this method, he abandoned his self imposed six minute "inside" time limit.

Plate (1975, p. 69) notes how he purchased a traveling alarm clock from a fence in Philadelphia. It was decorated with a basketball on top as the alarm bell. The clock also had the official team insignia of the Seattle Supersonics emblazoned across its face. We are not told where the clock came from. A personal interview by one of the authors with two members of a local college football team corroborated use of this method on a smaller scale. After their campus apartment was burglarized twice during home football games, the two roommates moved to an ethnic community in South Philadelphia.

This difficulty is all too familiar to celebrities outside the sports world. Hotel rooms of performers, for example, have traditionally been favorite targets during a performance. Use of known time blocks by average citizens was cleverly used in a well known scam practiced several years ago in Philadelphia. The technique was to first steal a car, one that did not have an especially high value in the stolen car market. The thieves would obtain the address of the owner from the contents of the car. A day later the car would be returned with a typewritten apology. The apology always explained that the car was sincerely needed for an "emergency." And would the owners "Please accept our apology and two tickets" to a current play? Finally, the house would be watched on the night of the performance, and burglarized if the owners left to attend the play.

Similar scams have been contrived in other areas. Obituaries, religious confirmations, and wedding announcements have all been used. In each case, the burglar is attempting to insure that the house will be unoccupied when the burglary attempt is made. A final example taken from a university setting is instructive. As it was reported in the faculty union newsletter (*APSCUF Newsletter*, 1984), "The faculty member, who was heavily in debt at the time, owed money to a person whom he later discovered had a long criminal record in another state. The person demanded payment in full immediately from the grievant, who was unable to borrow any more money. The grievant received numerous threats from his creditor which included burning down the grievant's farmhouse with his family in it. The grievant agreed to remove some university property and turn it over to his creditor. In addition, the grievant would supply him with names of colleagues and dates in which they would be out of town so their houses could be burglarized."

It is now obvious to us that if a house is to be unoccupied during known blocks of time, it must be secured in a way that makes entry a very lengthy effort. In this case, most burglars will choose another location. Most new housing in inner city areas provide examples of building design for internal security.

One of the surprising results of these interviews was the variety of intuitive logics expressed about time use. The intuition of most burglars about time use closely mirrors the findings of the BBC study and others (Shapcott and Steadman, 1978; Chapin, 1974). The burglars identified correctly the general trend of time use, although the details of their explanations were often wrong. This led most burglars to focus their criminal activity on times where there was a high probability that most suburbanites would not be home.

There are other burglars who do not subscribe to the same

intuition concerning time blocks. There are a few burglars who operate at what would seem to be all the wrong times. Dinner time, early morning, and even overnight all appeal to the intuition of someone. Not many of the burglars we interviewed operated at these times. Those few who did were able to find as many sites as they chose to burglarize. It seems no matter when you are away, there is a burglar with an idea about time use looking for your house.

Common sense precautions are very helpful, but seldom practiced. The best security for an empty house is an occupant. A house sitter or at least a house watcher should be used during vacation periods. The notificaton of trusted neighbors is the least one should do when away. The very wealthy are seldom burglarized because their houses are almost always occupied by a housekeeper. This provides security as an added benefit to the work performed. Many two career households will find full-time housekeepers practical. Although expensive, the housekeeper will be present during working hours when the residents are away. And there is always the appeal of relief from the drudgery of house cleaning and cooking. Many two career households may find a housekeeper well worth the cost.

Another attractive alternative for providing household security during working hours is to house share with a retired senior citizen. These individuals are very likely to be home during the day. Retired citizens are the best eyes and ears of security in residential areas during daylight hours.

We have seen how we can restructure the lives of residential burglars to deprive them of discretionary time when most homes are vacant. This is best done by requiring employment during probation and parole periods. Employment establishes positive habits of time use that encourage lawful activities after the correctional period. This, along with curfews, severely restrict the personal freedom of convicted individuals. However, these measures are much less restrictive than prison. As one participant in the Georgia intensive probation supervision program put it, "Anybody with any natural sense would rather do this than go to prison." (Gettinger, 1983, p.8). Rousseau (Cranston, 1968, p. 64) noted the need for individuals to subjugate their self interests to society, and the need of society to respond to those who are not able to conform when he wrote, "Hence, in order that the social pact shall not be an empty formula . . . whoever refuses to obey the general will shall be constrained to do so by the whole body, which means nothing other than that he shall be forced to be free."

We take time for granted. We tend not to notice how well ordered our lives are until a coincidence of events inconveniently reminds us. Our behavior is influenced by the way we use time and the constraints imposed on us by the availability of blocks of time. The typical burglar is more aware of our use of time than we are. Non-discretionary obligations take us away, and leave our homes vulnerable to residential burglary. We are all waiting to become victims of a burglar whose intuition about time use coincides with our routine. All that is left is for our burglar to locate us in space.

CHAPTER III

THE USE OF SPACE IN BURGLARY

Introduction

SUBURBAN residential burglary, unlike many urban crimes, requires several prior decisions. Many urban burglaries are spontaneous reactions to opportunities that present themselves during the course of daily activity. These spontaneous crimes are called situational crimes and occur while the burglar is working, or on his way to and from another activity. The only real decision is to seize the opportunity at hand.

Criminals in the suburbs face different conditions. They are not likely to just happen upon an unlocked door or other spontaneous opportunity. Suburban burglars usually need an automobile to reach the target area, and the decision to commit a burglary is usually made before they ever leave their homes. Suburban burglars must search for their opportunities.

Important Terms and Concepts

Suburban residential burglars must make at least two interrelated decisions to be in business (Rengert, 1980). The first is the basic decision to commit the crime. The second involves a decision about how and where to commit the crime. The decision about whether or not to commit a burglary has received the most research attention by criminologists. Their interest is

53

in what makes a person want to commit any crime, including burglary. The primary reason stated by the burglars we interviewed for deciding to commit a burglary was simply to obtain money. Without describing family background, demographic characteristics and socio-economic standing in detail, we can state that the need for money did not result from a struggle to feed and clothe a family. Many of these individuals were middle class or lower middle class, and many had employable skills. The need for money rose out of psychologically defined needs, not subsistence needs. These psychologically defined needs are things like a faster life style, drugs, and gambling. These activities demand more money than these people can earn legitimately. The decision to commit burglaries was a purposeful, rational decision in almost every case.

Our main concern here is the second question posed: Where is the burglary to be committed? We seek insight into how burglars choose a crime site. We want to know why they choose one area over the others available. The choice of a specific house rather than its neighbor will not be discussed here. This is a very idiosyncratic choice that will be touched on in the next chapter. Here, we are trying to understand the decisions made by burglars when they evaluate their environment. Environment in this sense includes the physical, social and economic infrastructure that the individual interacts with. Think of the environment as a stage on which the individual is an actor, and acts out his life without a predetermined script. The physical, economic and social factors are like the props and setting of the play.

This analogy makes it clear that the individual does not consider or perhaps even know about the environment beyond the stage where his life is acted out. In other words, people do not know all places equally well. People cannot evaluate places they have never visited or have no knowledge of. Proximity does not always equal familiarity.

Let's consider the relationship between spatial perception and the criminal use of space. The conceptual model of this relationship often used by geographers is useful to illustrate how space is perceived and used in different ways (Wolpert, 1964;

Brantingham and Brantingham, 1984, Chapter 12). Consider a large region, such as a metropolitan area or county as an example. Property criminals that are residential burglars cannot commit a crime unless they are aware of a location that provides an opportunity for burglary. This location is contained within the criminal's "awareness space" according to our model. The awareness space is the set of all places about which the criminal has some knowledge. Stated another way, it is a subset of the total regional environment.

The awareness space of a burglar contains places of varying utility for criminal exploitation. It is assumed that the criminal actively chooses among the available places within this awareness space. Not all places are considered. Only those places that are above a threshold or "breakeven" level of expectation for profitability and probability of success are considered. Several burglars laughed at even the suggestion of traveling to the city of Chester to perform a burglary. This is because of Chester's reputation as an economically distressed ghetto. One burglar even remarked, "You could get robbed in Chester."

Several black burglars flatly stated that the wealthy areas of Marple and Radnor were off limits for them. The risk for a black man in a "lily white" community was too great. Their presence alone would be noticed. Another burglar, also black, was not afraid of those areas. He went to great lengths to present himself in a context where he would not stand out. "You gotta dress for the occasion," as he put it. Dressed as a mover or workman driving a van or truck, he felt he had a high probability of success in areas of white wealth. The threshold varies and each burglar has his own rationale for evaluating the utility of an area.

The places that are above the threshold of profitability and safety form the criminal's "search space." The search space is a further subset of the criminal's awareness space. At each step, the field of potential areas for burglary become fewer.

Finally, within the criminal's search space is an area considered best or most comfortable for criminal activity. This chosen area is termed the "criminal activity space." It is the area actually exploited by the criminal. The criminal will continue

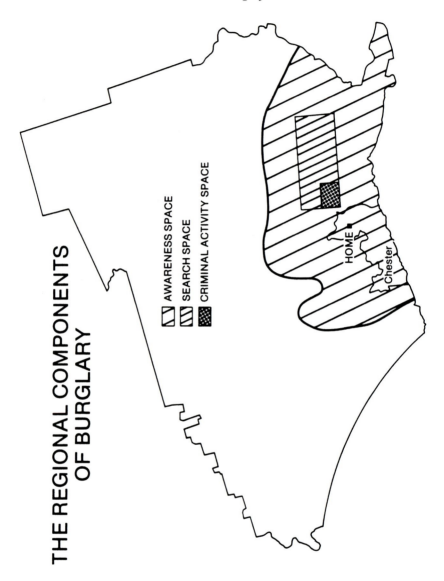

THE REGIONAL COMPONENTS OF BURGLARY

AWARENESS SPACE
SEARCH SPACE
CRIMINAL ACTIVITY SPACE

HOME

Chester

to operate in this area until he judges it no longer profitable, or too dangerous. Danger in this sense can come from fear of recognition, a change in policing patterns, or an intuitive feeling that luck is running out.

This model provides a useful way to sort out areas that

have burglary potential. Areas that have the same potential in an objective way may be judged by the burglar to have widely varying utility. This is because of the subjective nature of this process.

The model assumes that the criminal is actively engaged in the criminal evaluation and use of space. Because of this, the model will not be useful in evaluating the special cases of situational crimes and criminal opportunities discovered through secondary sources such as fences or friends.

The Use of Space in Crime

Let's turn our attention to a real world application of this conceptual model. It suggests a few questions, and as far as we can tell, criminals have never before been asked questions like these.

1) How much territory are criminals actually aware of;
2) How do criminals evaluate this territory for criminal purposes; and
3) How does the subjective spatial behavior of the criminals orient and direct the search for crime sites?

We mentioned previously that Delaware County is well suited from a spatial perspective for this kind of analysis. It is a diverse area with a wide range of neighborhood and community types. Many socio-economic groups are represented. Add to this the compact and accessible nature of the county. Major transportation arteries fan out over the county so that all areas are well served and easily reached. One can drive from one end of the county to the other in any direction in less than thirty minutes.

Almost all the burglars interviewed lived in one of two areas. The first cluster of burglars' residences is found in the southeastern corner of the county not far from the Philadelphia line. The second clustering is in the area in and around the city of Chester. Given the range of affluence and knowing where the burglars lived, it makes sense that there is strong economic incentive for these residential burglars to travel north in their search for a profitable burglary target. This situation is an almost ideal environmental laboratory to test ideas about the awareness and use of territory by residential burglars.

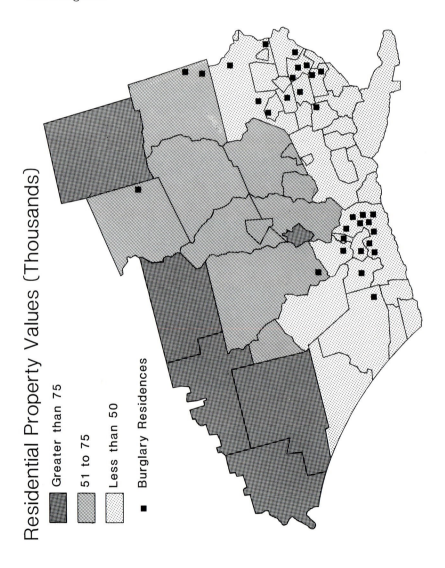

The Burglar's Awareness of Space

We can see that Delaware County offers a wide range of opportunities to a burglar, but what does the burglar see? The first step in our analysis is to determine how much of Delaware County our group of residential burglars is familiar with.

We measured the burglar's familiarity with different Delaware County locations through the use of a semantic differential scale. Each person interviewed was asked to rank each municipality and town in the county according to how well they knew the place on a scale of zero to ten. Interviewees were asked to rank their home area as ten, and places they had no knowledge of as zero. Every other area was then ranked with respect to these two reference points. The respondents were moderately familiar with about fifty per cent of the places in the county, although there was considerable spatial clustering of known places in the southern part of the county. Generally, burglars were most familiar with areas close to their home, and these were clustered in the southern and southeastern parts of the county. The only exceptions were Media and Thornbury Township for obvious reason. Media is the county seat and location of Common Pleas court, and Thornbury Township is the location of the prison. There was a clear decline in familiarity as these burglars were asked about other places in the north of Delaware County.

The Burglars' Evaluation of Space

The next step in our analysis is to examine how burglars evaluated the places they had knowledge of as potential burglary sites. In this analysis, we asked the burglar to evaluate only those areas that he was familiar with, using a rating scale. Ten on the scale was assigned to the location felt to be the best in the county for residential burglary, and one was given to the worst place. Zero was assigned to places they had no knowledge of and was excluded from the scaling analysis. All other places were rated between one and ten.

Again, we see distances from the southern part of the county as important. The southernmost part of the county was

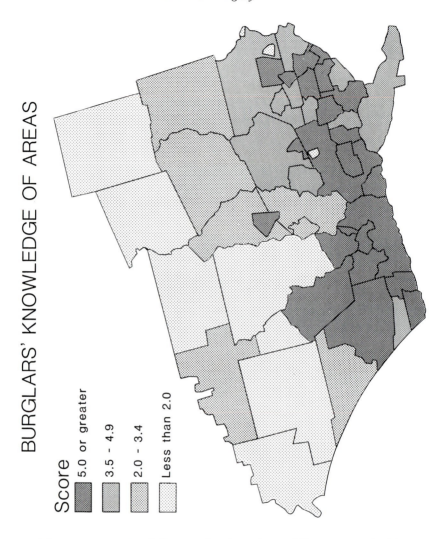

rated low as a potential area for burglary. We expected this, based on low property values. The highest ranked areas surprisingly are not the most affluent areas. The highest ranking went to areas in the tier of mid-priced housing just outside the home area of the burglars. An exception is well known, affluent Radnor Township located in the northernmost part of the county. Radnor was rated very high by those burglars who

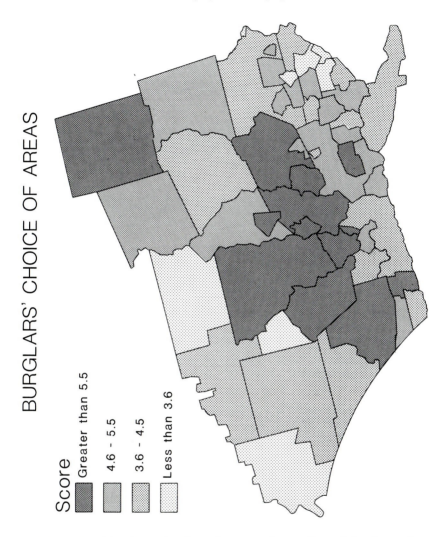

BURGLARS' CHOICE OF AREAS

Score

Greater than 5.5

4.6 - 5.5

3.6 - 4.5

Less than 3.6

had heard of it, but the burglars we interviewed had rarely committed a burglary there. The high ranked areas close to home, though not as rich as Radnor, were far more popular as burglary sites. These areas were those most often burglarized by the interviewees during their burglary careers. It seems that distance and familiarity are as important as economic consideration in the criminal evaluation of places (Reppetto, 1974; Scarr; 1973; Cohen and Cantor, 1981).

Cultural perceptions also play an important role in the criminal evaluation of areas (Morrill, 1965). "You'll get shot if you're caught there," was a common response of blacks with respect to white housing areas, and whites with respect to black housing areas. Everyone was cautious toward Marcus Hook and Trainer. These areas were heavily populated by motorcycle gangs in the recent past. The burglars were especially afraid of the "Pagans," the local motorcycle gang. Several burglars described graphically what they thought would happen to them if the house they happened to break into was occupied by a "Pagan." A local gang can provide protection to a community from criminals living outside their residential area (Ley, 1974).

As described in the introduction, a cultural barrier to spatial movement in physical form seems to be West Chester Pike, Route 3. Although the highway can be crossed easily, it seems to act as a perceptual dividing line between northern and southern parts of the county. There seems to be relatively little social interaction between residents living north and south of the highway. For instance, until recently most of the high schools south of Route 3 did not play high schools north of Route 3 in sports. The affluent areas north of the highway resemble the adjoining areas of Chester and Montgomery Counties much more than areas closer, but south of Route 3. The wealth, style and attitudes of the Main Line flow north and west. Areas south of Route 3 are middle class in every way and are more oriented to Philadelphia as a social and work center. Farther south and nearer the Delaware River are the distinctive blue collar industrial communities. In short, Route 3, although easily crossed, seems to divide the county culturally into a northern and southern part. Using Lynch's terminology, these are two different "districts" and Route 3 is the "edge" (Lynch, 1960).

This led us to question what really attracts criminals to specific search areas. We began to consider the burglars' possible sources of information, and how they learned about space to better understand this decision.

Learning About Space

Spatial perception is the awareness of two dimensional extended space in the form of the world around us. Spatial awareness is the result of a learning process encompassing a variety of information sources (Golledge, 1981). This learning process may be either active or passive depending upon the information source. Passive spatial learning occurs as spatial knowledge is accrued through day to day activities. The purpose of these activities can be anything in our daily lives except exploring new areas to gain spatial knowledge. In everyday activities such as traveling to work, shopping or a social occasion, we passively assimilate spatial information. We learn quickly about new road construction when it affects our regular route to work, although we don't travel the route specifically to determine road conditions.

Passive learning journeys are characterized by habit (Pipkin, 1981). These are journeys that are traveled regularly and by force of habit. Studies show that when an individual changes jobs or moves, they seldom try more than three alternatives before they settle on a specific route that becomes routine (Hensher, 1976). Changes to this travel pattern are resisted after this habitual route has been decided. Notice how quickly many people become irritated on their way to work if they are forced off a familiar route by road construction or some other barrier. We tend to avoid the unfamiliar in our journeys through space.

Relatively little additional spatial knowledge is gained after the initial exploration to find the best route. Any spatial knowledge gained is gained passively while completing the journey. We tend to ignore spatial information around us unless something unusual gets in the way. One might wonder how passive journeys are important to criminal activity. The habitual spatial paths of passive journeys tend to directionally orient criminal activity. As we will demonstrate, this occurs even when information from these spatial journeys is not directly used in criminal activity.

When starting on a journey, we tend to be directionally

ACTION AND SEARCH SPACES

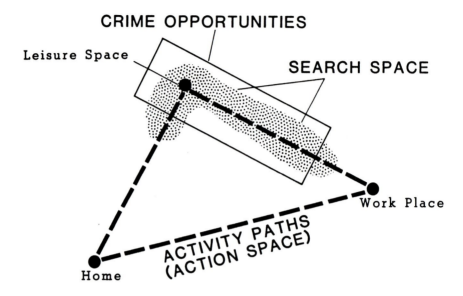

oriented by familiar paths even when we set out to explore unfamiliar areas. For example, many of us have had the experience of starting out on a Sunday drive and, without noticing, found ourselves half way to our work place. Another example commonly occurs when we are driving to a destination in the same direction as our work place, and we forget to turn toward our destination. Again, we wind up most of the way to a place we had no intention of going. The automobile seems singleminded. In short, familiar habitual journeys tend to direct even unfamiliar journeys in familiar directions.

This brings us to the second way indviduals obtain spatial knowledge — tnrough the active evaluation and exploration of space. The whole purpose of spatial activity in the active learning process is to obtain information for later use. The environment is actively examined or cased and evaluated for its usefulness. This may entail entering unfamiliar areas. In this case, the process is termed "spatial exploration."

Unfamiliar territory is entered either by extending a known

activity path into unfamiliar territory or by traveling in a different direction that leads to new places at shorter distances. In either case, the environment is actively evaluated for its utility for the purpose in mind, whether criminal or noncriminal. This evaluation process is the same for criminal activity as it would be for determining the best location for a fast food restaurant. We will show that for criminal activity individuals tend to extend familiar habitual paths, rather than travel in an unfamiliar direction.

Secondary sources of information are a special case. Individuals obtain spatial information from secondary sources such as friends, the media, working partners or fences. These information sources do not depend on the past spatial knowledge of the individual to orient the direction of spatial activity. The knowledge of the new location is a "chance location" from the perspective of the spatial actor. Previous spatial behavior of the individual gives us few clues as to the probable location of the new spatial knowledge. There is no identifiable probability of the direction or distance of the spatial location from the individual. The new location is almost a shot in the dark compared to the order and structure of our learned spatial knowledge.

This model of behavior puts criminal spatial activity into perspective for those cases where the criminal is actively engaged in the criminal evaluation and use of space. It is less useful in interpreting situational crimes. These crimes are opportunities that present themselves to the criminal in the course of everyday events, and are just too good to pass up. Situational crimes are not actively sought out, and there is usually no planning involved. These crimes are located well within the individual's daily activity space in most cases.

A recent incident provides a good example. Joey Coyle had not set out to commit a crime, or even considered the possibility when he happened upon a cash bag from an armored car lying in the middle of the intersection of Wolf and Swanson in south Philadelphila. The bag contained 1.2 million dollars in unmarked one hundred dollar bills. The money had just fallen from the back of an armored car, unnoticed by the guards. As the armored car drove away, Coyle could not resist. The op-

portunity was just too great. He scooped up the sack of money
and disappeared.

The Philadelphia Police followed every anonymous tip,
and even used a hypnotist to elicit information from by-
standers in the area at the time. Every bar bill paid with a one
hundred dollar bill was considered a lead. A big break came
when Coyle entered the wrong house in New Jersey, boasting
in a loud voice about his new wealth. When Coyle discovered
his mistake, he apologized and gave the amazed residents of
the home several hundred dollars on his way out. This led to a
thorough description of Coyle. Finally, after a lengthy investigation, Coyle was apprehended at Kennedy International Air-
port in New York. He was waiting to board a flight for
Mexico. He had over $100,000 in one hundred dollar bills
stuffed in his boots.

His plea at trial was that the sight of all that money made
him temporarily insane. As an aside, Mr. Coyle was found not
guilty, and over $100,000 of the money was never found. Al-
though the incident took place along one of his familiar activity
paths, the crime did not depend on his spatial knowledge. The
crime was a chance occurrence. Ironically, the clue that led to
his apprehension was an equally chance occurrence, and a
very unfortunate mistake in space use for Mr. Coyle (Larson,
1981).

A final consideration is the style of the very best burglars.
These criminals rely heavily on research rather than spatial
search (Cohen and Cantor, 1981). Individuals or wealthy
neighborhoods are selected, and the individual's behavior
studied. The burglar strikes when the resident is away and the
conditions are right. The methods used are those appropriate
to the site, and not the burglar's routine method. Site, timing
and method are all chosen as a result of analysis of the target.
As we mentioned earlier, one of Philadelphia's sports teams
was the target for such a burglar. These burglars are extremely
analytical and thorough in their work. They are almost impossible to stop, if you are their target. Fortunately for us all,
burglars of this brilliance are rare.

Clearly, we need to understand the nature of the information source used by the criminal to locate a criminal activity site if we hope to make sense of the spatial pattern of crime occurrences. Consider the distance from the criminal's home to the crime site. We can conceptualize the probable location of the crime. Closest to home will be situational crimes happened upon during the criminal's daily activities. Next are crime opportunities located through the criminal's evaluation of places he knows about. Finally, the farthest are crime opportunities located through spatial exploration. Randomly distributed among and along this continuum are criminal opportunities identified by fences or friends.

These are some of the relationships between spatial learning and criminal behavior suggested by the information we gathered from active burglars. We have already established the amount of space the burglars are aware of, and how they evaluate its crime potential through the use of ratings. Next, we would like to break down some of this information by the burglar's source of information. This comparison of crime site, spatial knowledge and information source will illustrate clearly how active and passive information sources shape the spatial form of criminal activity. Emphasis will fall on the journey to work because of its influence in determining the likely direction of criminal activity from the burglar's residence. As stated by Pipkin (1981, p. 148), "The work-trip is numerically the most important trip for most adults."

Relationship of Crime to Non-Criminal Spatial Activity

When we began this chapter, we suggested that the non-criminal use of space would affect the criminal evaluation and use of space. In other words, it is daily activities like traveling to work or school that orients criminals toward crime sites and helps them choose those with the best potential. In order to test this notion, we needed information on the daily use of space for both criminal and non-criminal activities. We gathered this information from the daily diaries, mentioned in the previous chapter, that we asked the burglars to construct. Each individual traced a typical day starting with the time they awoke in the morning through to the time they went to bed at night. They described hour by hour the typical activities that they habitually completed during the day. Almost every prisoner enjoyed recalling better times. We were often struck by the sharp contrast between the freedom they described and the austere discipline of the prison. For several individuals, we were saddened by the emptiness of their lives. Reconstructing their lives outside the prison was not a difficult task because daily life is habit forming. Most prisoners seemed to genuinely enjoy describing their life outside the prison.

This information allowed us to identify work places and habitual travel paths to work for those who had held jobs during the year prior to their conviction. We were also able to identify weekend recreation areas and routes traveled to these locations. Work places are easy to identify because in most cases they do not vary from day to day. Recreation sites vary, but in almost all cases, the immediate response was something like, "On Saturday, I usually go to the park and drink a few beers with my buddies," or an equally explicit response. We accepted this response as typical and representative of the individual's leisure activites. We used these responses to locate each individual's leisure activities.

Orientation of Crime Sites to Work Places

Now we know where the burglar lived, worked, and spent his leisure time. We also know the location of each burglar's crime sites. We took the latter information from the District Attorney's records. The first question pursued with this information was the spatial relationship between the work places and the burglary sites. To test this spatial relationship for each burglar interviewed, burglary sites were plotted on a map along with the home of the burglar. To measure the distance and directional orientation of the crime sites, a protractor was placed on the map with the zero axis set on the home-work place direction. The direction of the burglary sites can then be measured with respect to this axis. One hundred and eighty degrees would be a crime site located in the opposite direction from the work place and ninety degrees would be at right angles to the home-work place axis. The distance of the work place of each employed interviewee is measured along the zero axis and the distance to each burglary site is scaled in the direction it occurred with respect to the home-work axis (Adams, 1969).

There is a marked orientation of the crime sites in the direction of the work place. Visually, this is very clear. Thirty-one of the forty burglary sites of fourteen burglars who had worked within a year of their conviction are located in the quartile between zero and forty-five degrees. This directional bias implies that the search behavior of the burglars is oriented, if not constrained, by the habitual, familiar journey to work. Many of the crime sites were just beyond the work place. Many were located just off the familiar path from home to work. We feel this implies that the burglar's search may extend the familiar path to work, or veer off it at some point along the way. In either case, the burglar is strongly influenced by the direction of his work place in his search for a crime site.

Orientation of Crime Sites to Recreation Places

We can use the same information to examine the influence of recreation places. Recreation places are plotted for the thirteen burglars who were not employed within a year of their conviction, but actively searched for crime locations. We noticed that routes to recreation sites tend to be longer on the average than routes to work for our group of suburban burglars. This is opposite to the relationship found by Chapin in Washington, D.C. (1974).

Again, we notice a directional bias of burglary sites compared to the journey to recreation places; but there is less clustering of burglary sites in the home-recreation axis than in the home-work axis. Twenty of thirty-five burglary sites were located between zero and forty-five degrees of this axis. It seems that both work and recreation travel tend to orient the direction of the burglar's search behavior. However, the direction of the work place seems more important than the direction of the recreation place.

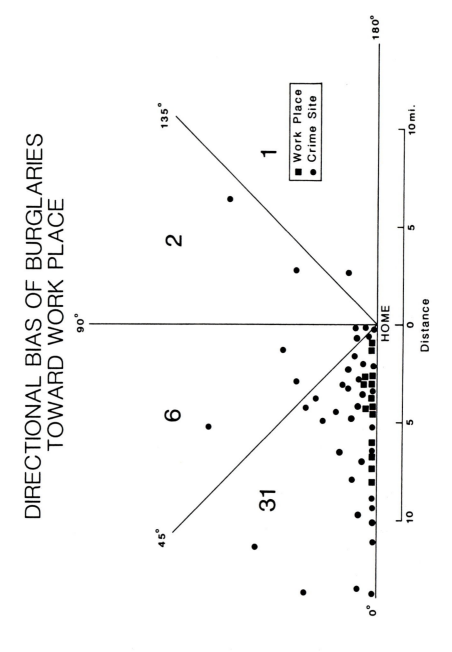

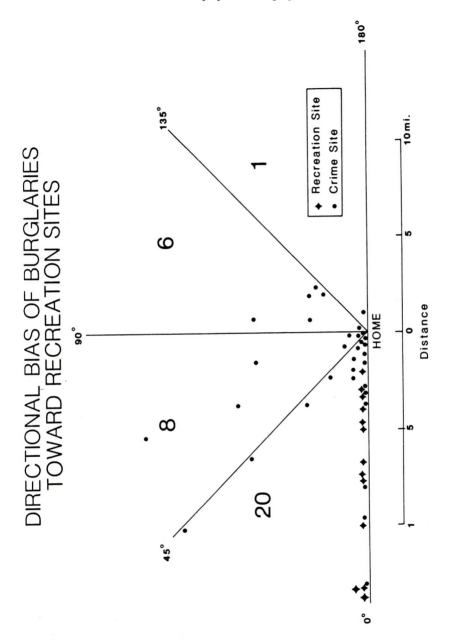

DIRECTIONAL BIAS OF BURGLARIES
TOWARD RECREATION SITES

Orientation Through Secondary Information Sources

Finally, we can compare these spatial patterns with a natural control group: individuals who did not use their own spatial knowledge because they used secondary sources to identify crime sites. In other words, a fence, the media, a friend or some other source told them about a site, and the burglar's own search never even began. Second hand spatial information results in a much more randomly distributed spatial pattern of burglary sites than a first hand search. The average distance from home is also somewhat longer. There are fewer places clustered near the home of the burglar.

When secondary information sources are used, crime sites are located in all directions and at greater distances from the burglar's home. Comparing the spatial patterns of active search and secondary information sources for locating crime sites confirms for us the idea that habitual travel influences nonhabitual travel. People tend to start off in familiar directions even if they are going into unfamiliar territory. And they tend to minimize the distance necessary to locate their objective. In this case, intervening opportunities are utilized. In other words, when these burglars have a choice, they use closer rather than more distant crime sites.

There is always the possibility in an analysis of this type that the results will be misleading. This is a concern here because of the number of people interviewed and the ideal nature of Delaware County as a setting. We felt more comfortable about the home-work result after working on the home-recreation information. After reviewing the home-secondary source site axis, we are confident that all the results are genuine. We look forward to replicating the test with a larger sample in another area.

Summary and Conclusions

It seems clear from this analysis that many of the assumptions used in aggregate models do not hold for our group of residential burglars. For example, these people are not familiar with all the area around them. They do not give equal con-

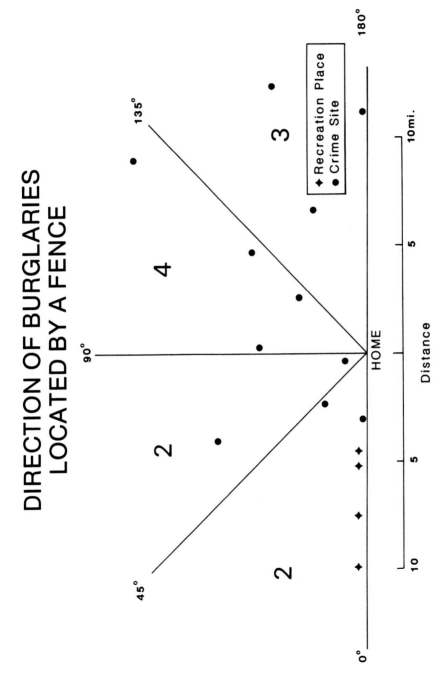

sideration to all the area they are aware of in their criminal evaluation of space. They are guided by past travel habits. Finally, a large group of property criminals have their criminal spatial decisions made for them by fences and others. Their situation, spatially, may be relatively trivial in predicting the probable location of their crime sites.

It's interesting to note that some burglars did not always use the information they had. Those burglars from the southernmost areas of the county who knew about places like Radnor still preferred the closer tier of mid-priced housing to the wealthier part of the county. One impression we were left with is that these burglars are comfortable burglarizing people one social class up from themselves. Those in blue collar areas burglarized middle class neighborhoods. The only burglars we interviewed who operated on the wealthy Main Line were themselves from middle class and upper middle class areas like Haverford and Newtown Townships.

Work and recreation places seem to orient the direction of the search for burglars actively searching for crime locations. Recent trends in metropolitan transportation will bring about change and possibly increase the suburban crime rate by increasing everyone's awareness space. The suburbanization of industry has brought many blue collar employees who traditionally live in inner city areas out to the industrial parks of the suburbs (Muller, 1981). These are people who may have had no prior knowledge of the suburbs and will expand their awareness space dramatically. The suburban shopping mall attracts customers from a wide area and draws them to a local suburban area. This again expands the awareness space of those who learn a new travel path. Property crime rates can be expected to rise in localities that have attractions such as these. Further, little known suburban areas that are relatively crime free can be expected to experience more crime as a greater number of people become familiar with these outlying areas.

These considerations highlight the ethical considerations of identifying and strengthening barriers to criminal spatial mobility. When crime is displaced from one area to another, rates rise and fall. Politicians and policy makers often confuse displacing crime with attacking the problem of what causes the decision to engage in criminal activity in the first place.

When crime is displaced into a relatively low income area that is economically less capable of combatting crime, there is a temptation to "write off" the area and the problem. For example, inner city criminals sometimes get more lenient sentences than suburban criminals for the same crime (Epstein, 1978). This can be interpreted as the judicial system "writing off" the inner city while protecting suburban or more affluent areas. Inner city areas suffer a higher crime rate than suburban areas partly through the false economy of spending less for imprisonment and rehabilitation than the suburban areas. The attitude of many suburban residents is that the higher urban crime rate is somehow "natural" and to be expected. This deflects concern away from the victims of inner city crimes and focuses it on how to keep crime from *spreading* to the suburbs. Obviously, victims of crime should receive consideration equally, without regard to where they live. Ironically, continued concern for how to stop the spread of crime, rather than how to alleviate criminogenic situations, almost insures that crime will diffuse out into previously safe areas.

During the course of interviewing, a baseball story came to mind because it so aptly described the search behavior of burglars. "Hit 'em where they ain't" is how Wee Willie Keeler described successful batting in baseball. It is a comment that describes well a burglar's intuitive consideration of both time and space.

CHAPTER IV

THE TECHNIQUES OF BURGLARY

MANY THINGS go into a burglary. When a burglar is at work, there is an interaction between his intent, his knowledge of the area and his ability to predict when his target is unprotected. This chapter is the burglar's approach to burglary. Here, the techniques of burglary will be discussed. Beginning with the method of planning prior to a burglary trip, we proceed through a discussion of burglary site selection, means of entering a residence, routine followed once inside the house, and finally a look at where our burglars went wrong and were apprehended. This will provide a profile of the process of burglary from planning to execution to apprehension. Our purpose is to glimpse what goes on in a burglar's mind; how decisions are made; how habits are formed; how mistakes are made; and finally, what goes so wrong that they are caught and convicted.

Method of Planning

The amount of planning that goes into a residential burglary varies from very little to a very careful consideration of which house to burglarize, how to establish if the resident is at home, method of entry and where within the house the valuables might be located. Little or no preliminary planning is usually associated with burglaries committed by amateur criminals, called "cowboys" by the professionals. Most of the unplanned ventures are initiated when a burglar happens upon an opportunity he finds too good to pass up during his daily activities. In some cases, the burglar is constantly on the watch for an opportunity to steal something. This is the case in many low income areas where the tendency toward crime may be high. In any case, it is the perception of the opportunity that leads to the criminal activity: the how and the why are obvious after the burglary opportunity is spotted. In simplest form, this type of burglary is referred to as "smash and grab." As the name suggests, this is a situation where the burglar notices something of value near a window or door that can be broken. The burglar smashes out the glass, takes the object and runs without ever actually entering the residence.

Other instances closely related are burglaries carried out when the resident is running an errand or in the garden, and the burglar notices an open front door. Here again, the opportunity is viewed as too good to pass up. In the criminological literature, crimes that result from little or no prior planning are termed "situational crimes" or "opportunity crimes" (Brantingham and Brantingham, 1984). Simple common sense and care on the part of residents can alleviate most of these crimes.

Carefully planned burglaries are characteristic of highly professional burglars who are well versed in their craft. Carefully planned burglaries are difficult to control, and some methods of burglary are almost impossible to prevent. Many of these methods are learned and passed on by word of mouth, often within the prison where such topics form a common area of interest that can safely be discussed between inmates. The professional techniques of the burglar form the *modus operandi* — that is the behavior pattern followed in succeeding burglaries. If it is not altered over time, this pattern can become a significant clue that allows the police to link burglaries to the same burglar and eventually lead to apprehension. The elite burglar carefully plans ahead to alter any emerging *modus operandi* before a pattern can be associated with his crimes in any specific area.

This pattern is not always a single clue as usually portrayed on television. Most often, it is a combination of obvious actions that form the modus operandi and link several burglaries to the same burglar. For example, many burglars use pillow cases to carry away valuables. Some will ransack a site, and some leave it undisturbed. A pillow case, a neat and tidy crime scene and a jimmied window when found in more than one burglary can indicate one burglar's work. Police can often go into further detail by looking at the pry marks on a forced door jam or window frame. Are they narrow and deep or broad and flat? This tells about the tool used to enter. Narrow pry marks are from a screwdriver, and broad from a chisel or prybar. Sometimes it's chance, but sometimes it's a burglar with a favorite tool. One energetic burglar we interviewed had a special "key to the city" prybar forged by a friend. The marks left by this tool were distinctive and a modus operandi on their own merit.

Criminal planning can also be categorized by the information sources used. Situational crimes, described above, are the result of information or opportunity just happened upon in the normal course of the burglar's daily life. A slight variation of this theme is the case of "part time" burglars. These are low income individuals who are not full time criminals, but turn to crime in times of need. The loss of a job, Christmas or a birthday force these individuals who earn just enough, to supplement their income through burglary. The burglar in these circumstances goes down to the corner or other hangout, and asks to "get in on whatever's happening." There, among local acquaintances, information is exchanged and various scenarios are discussed. We refer to this on-the-spot planning as "street corner planning." Typically, this kind of occasional need for money precedes any concrete plans to use crime as a way to obtain money. Friends and acquaintances are queried for good ideas and join in speculation about various possibilities.

At a more regular and professional level are burglars who discover opportunities through fences and other criminal contacts. Sometimes these criminal relationships of cooperation are longstanding. The fence generally has inside information that takes most of the uncertainty out of the burglary. Fences know where the valuables are or when houses are unguarded. In one case, a burglar was getting information from a police officer. The officer told the burglar which homes were being given special attention because the residents had notified the police department of their vacation plans. In another case, a fence identified synagogues with religious artifacts of gold and silver. There is a division of responsibilities when a burglar works with a fence. One specializes in identifying the opportunities, and the other, the mechanics of the actual burglary. Planning is a twofold process, and each individual works only in their own realm.

Some burglars we interviewed worked with fences who acted more like brokers. Instead of identifying the exact house to be burglarized, they only identified goods they had a ready market for. It's up to the burglar to decide where and how to obtain the goods. Commonly, this type of planning takes place at a local bar where word is passed that someone needs a new stereo or a camera. The fence matches buyer and seller, and the seller is the burglar.

A final form of fencing described to us was the fence who buys all stolen goods that have a resale value. These are not presold and must be warehoused. This is a favorable situation for the burglar because, although prices paid are discounted, the burglar can rely upon quickly disposing of the stolen goods. Most burglars favor quick cash and rapid disposal of potential evidence. The disadvantages to the fence are obvious. Most people do not have 5 VCRs and 12 televisions in their garages. Owners of "second hand" shops are frequently inspected by local police on the lookout for stolen goods. Fences that use this cover must keep goods that are obviously stolen in a backroom or at another location. Shop operators that do not participate in illegal activity must be constantly on the lookout to avoid accepting stolen goods that could be seized as evidence.

The modus opeandi is also the planning process for some professional burglars. These burglars have established a method of operation that they use time and again. These burglars are very active, and sometimes strike several times a day. Each burglary is a run through of the burglar's established, tried and true routine in a new location. The greatest danger lies in becoming careless in the execution of a reliable plan. For example, some burglars will spend up to an hour to be sure that their car is ready and in good working order. Their greatest fear is to be stopped with a car full of stolen goods by the local police because a tail light is burned out, or some equally trivial mechanical problem. One burglar was apprehended because a police officer stopped to assist him when his tire went flat. The burglar had already taken the jack from the trunk, but could not open the trunk for the spare tire without revealing the stolen goods to the helpful officer. The really good burglar is very careful to minimize these risks by thoroughly checking his equipment.

A second danger for a professional burglar who follows an established plan is that a perceptive police force will soon identify the pattern and link several burglaries. Burglars often like to work a specific neighborhood or area until something happens to make the burglar feel there is increased risk in further activity. Things like being seen close enough to be identified, or having a conspicuous incident with the car are circumstances that make the burglar feel his luck is running out. Several close encounters with the local police usually signal increased surveillance, directed patrol and time for the burglar to move on. Although things like these call for a change, it is usually a change in location, and not a change in the burglar's routine.

The amount of planning for a residential burglary varies from little or none for situational crimes, to elaborate, carefully detailed and refined plans characteristic of the most professional burglar. Sometimes, planning is the effort of several people. In other cases, the entire planning process is the work of a single individual. In either case, practice makes perfect, and the individuals become more skillful over time.

Many burglars learn the hard way. The early years of their careers are spent in jail as a result of mistakes due to inexperience. Mistakes are less frequent as the burglar becomes more professional. As burglars become more experienced and professional, their mistakes often become more costly. A simple mistake, when coupled with a previous record, will put an experienced burglar back in prison. One part of burglary, the site selection process, is examined in some detail. The critical issue of burglary, certainly from the victim's point of view, is site selection. Or, put another way, why my house and not my neighbors?

Site Selection — What a Burglar Looks for in a House

Most of us are very concerned about becoming a victim of crime. People take elaborate precautions ranging from burglar alarms to watch dogs to protect their homes and property. Seldom are we aware of what catches a burglar's attention in choosing a home to burglarize. We are only familiar with the obvious clues used by opportunistic burglars to find unoccupied homes. We should not let mail pile up in our mailboxes and newspapers pile up on our front steps when we are on vacation. We shouldn't leave a ladder leaning against the house while we're away. A timer to turn lights and a radio on and off during early evening hours while we are away is a good idea. These are a few of the obvious clues and precautions people generally think of as a way of putting off potential burglars.

These clues are only the obvious ones that provide evidence of an unoccupied home. The experienced burglar often looks for less obvious clues; ones we tend to overlook in securing our homes. One burglar mentioned that he especially liked to drive slowly through residential neighborhoods on very hot days. Closed windows and air conditioners that were not running were his signal that a home was unguarded. Most people turn air conditioners off when away to conserve energy. Most people would never think of air conditioning as a clue for a prowling burglar.

One of the burglars we interviewed told us his method of locating unoccupied homes was to follow a school bus for a few blocks through a residential community. He noted the cars parked in the driveways. Thirty minutes or so later, he passed through the neighborhood again and noted where the cars were now gone. These were homes where a parent had waited for the arrival of the bus to run an afternoon errand or leave for work in the morning. In any event, the house was probably empty and a good candidate for burglary. Another burglar drove around residential neighborhoods between 9:00 and 10:00 on Sunday morning and watched for families leaving for church.

These are just a few of the visual clues used by burglars to locate a home temporarily unoccupied. There are as many clues as there are burglars and too many to mention here. Instead, we will point out some of the non-visual methods used to locate unguarded homes. Some are well known and others more subtle.

Probably the best known technique is to use the telephone book to locate empty houses. A burglar can scan the telephone directory or look up a name from a mailbox and simply dial the home. If someone answers, the burglar simply hangs up and tries another number. This has led many residents in affluent ares with a high potential for burglary to use unlisted numbers. Another means of confusing the burglar is to have a phone answering machine. In this case, the burglar cannot be sure you are not at home because many people leave the machine on when they are home, but too busy to answer.

Another means of locating potentially unguarded homes is through funeral notices published in newspapers. Burglars realize that this is a time when family and friends of the deceased are likely to be at the funeral. This method of locating unguarded homes is especially ghoulish, but successful. Many of the burglars we interviewed mentioned this trick, but none would admit to using it themselves. Each had "heard about it" from another criminal. Close relatives should arrange to have someone stay in or watch their homes while at the funeral. Of course, the home of the deceased should be included in these precautions. There is little honor among thieves.

In Delaware County, there are ten local papers, mostly weeklies, in addition to the Philadelphia Inquirer and Daily News. The small local papers offer a wealth of neighborhood news including the vacation and travel news about local residents. These notices often include exact dates of the trip. This is less expensive, but just as effective as an advertisement notifying residential burglars that you are not at home. Many suburban residents use house sitters to live in and protect their home while they are away.

We have already mentioned in the chapter about time the unusual circumstances of college and professional athletes, entertainers, local celebrities and politicians. These are a few of the people in our community that are especially vulnerable to crimes at their residences because they cannot avoid advertising their whereabouts when they are away from home.

A final means of obtaining knowledge of unguarded homes is through information gathered while performing a legitimate occupation. One burglar we talked to, Burglar #18, worked for a well-established landscaping and lawncare firm. During the course of the afternoon he would ask the property owner for "something cold to drink." If they invited him in, as most people did, he would note the layout of the house and the location of any valuable articles. He would also notice the habitual goings and comings of the residents. If the house was left unguarded at a specific time each day, he made a mental note of the pattern. Then, a couple of weeks after he finished the landscaping work, he would return and put this information to work by burglarizing the home.

A similar method was used by a roofer. He would watch the travel habits of an entire neighborhood and burglarize homes that were unguarded. Delivery work is another legitimate occupation frequently used to gather information for criminal activity. A wise precaution is to alter regular travel habits when people are working in the vicinity of your home or property. Stay home as much as possible and return home at irregular intervals during the day to check on your home if you must be away while workmen are in the area. This is another instance where retired individuals who are home during the day can keep a watchful eye on an entire neighborhood.

An occupation frequently used by burglars to case homes is that of salesman. Articulate burglars need only a clipboard and pen to become salesmen, pollsters with "a few questions for the lady of the house", or an inspector of some sort. Clipboard in hand, the burglar goes door to door. Ideally, no one is home and the front door is unlocked. If a resident comes to the door, the burglar assumes his other identity and does his best to talk his way inside to case the house. Always be wary of anyone going door to door. Never hesitate to call the police and ask them to check a salesman's credentials. Whenever possible, sales people should be kept at the front door. Never allow a salesperson in more than one room of the house, preferably the entryway or livingroom.

There are several situational clues used by burglars to identify a specific house to enter. If a house does not jump out at the burglar for a good reason, burglars generally choose a corner property. Corner houses offer more avenues of escape and better visibility than houses in the middle of a street. Corner properties only have one or two close neighbors. They are less likely to be watched by neighbors than a home with neighbors on each side, as well as behind and across the street.

In fact, burglars seem to have intuitively sensed what social theorists have found to be true. Persons living in the center of a block are more likely to have high levels of neighbor interaction than people who live at the corners. Whyte even went so far as to suggest that introverts should occupy end properties, and extroverts, properties in mid-block (Whyte, 1956). This is another indication that residents of corner properties will receive less assistance and concern from neighbors than those who live in the middle of friendly blocks. Finally, residents of corner properties are usually more accustomed to strangers than middle of the street residents. This is because strangers lost in residential areas tend to ask for directions and assistance at crossroads where a choice must be made. Victimization studies consistently confirm that corner properties are the most vulnerable to burglary (Brantingham and Brantingham, 1984).

Street layout is also an important consideration in residential burglary. Burglars do not like to be inconvenienced in selecting houses to burglarize. Their driving behavior is much like that of a joy rider "just cruising around." They do not like to attract attention to themselves by turning or backtracking, and several types of streets require this. In an important study of the relationship of street patterns to residential burglary, Bevis and Nutter (1977) demonstrated that burglary victimization is closely related to the degree of access afforded by street design. They identified five types of street design. In increasing order of accessibility these are: (1) dead end streets; 2) cul-de-sacs; 3) L shaped streets; 4) T shaped streets; and 5) cross streets. Burglary rates were then measured for each type of street in Minneapolis, Minnesota. The results are clear. Streets that are easiest to drive through (not into) are the streets that burglars chose as burglary sites. Burglary rates are higher on a cross sreet than in a cul-de-sac.

Other studies have demonstrated that houses near a major highway (within a block or two) are more likely to be selected as burglary targets than houses farther away (Rengert and Wasilchick, 1980; Luedtke, 1970). Burglars do not want to travel farther from a familiar highway than is necessary to locate a good site to burglarize. If the burglar becomes familiar with the area through his job, perhaps as a delivery truck driver, then the extended street network becomes more familiar. As the street network becomes more familiar, the burglary sites may be spread around this extended location.

Two generalizations can be made. If the burglar is unfamiliar with the immediate area, he is likely to locate a site within a block or two of a major highway leading in and out of the area. If the burglar is familiar with the surrounding area, more secluded sites may be selected as burglary targets. In either case, if a car is used in the burglary, the burglar is likely to pick a through street rather than a dead end or a cul-de-sac.

A rule of thumb for a burglar is to pick a house with as few close neighbors as possible. Not only corner properties, but also properties that back onto open or unused land are desirable. This unused land can be fields or wooded areas. The ideal situation from the burglar's point of view is for this land to generate pedestrian traffic. Parkland, golf courses, school grounds and industrial property are especially enticing because they place a lot of unfamiliar people in the neighborhood. The potential burglar can blend into the unfamiliar faces drawn into the area and feign a legitimate reason for being in the neighborhood.

In the case of open fields or unused land, a stranger walking across this area might attract more attention. Wooded and overgrown areas where burglars are less visible are preferred in this situation. It provides a good escape route if it is needed, and partially shrouds one side of the house from the view of neighbors. One of the wonders of suburban architecture is that this side of the house usually has large sliding glass doors that open onto a secluded patio. It is as if the home was designed for the benefit of the criminal rather than the security of the resident.

A home with overgrown shrubbery is another situation sought out by burglars. The shrubbery hides the burglar from the view of neighbors and passersby. This visual seclusion provides a sense of security for the criminal as he works to enter the house. The burglar is not easily seen even if he is simply ringing the doorbell to establish that no one is home. Nothing is more disconcerting to a burglar than to have a nosey neighbor happen by to tell him no one is at home. "Old guys," one burglar told us, "they're the worst because that's all they do is watch their neighbors." Most burglars we talked to said that after a face to face contact like this, they would leave the area immediately.

Some burglars are as concerned with signs that indicate which homes are worth burglarizing as they are with searching for homes with the right surroundings that make them easy and safe to burglarize. There are certain signs that burglars have learned to read that indicate the homeowner has things of value. Antiques prominently displayed in a window or on the porch is a good indicator that there is more and better inside.

A person who displays a restored church pew, a spinning wheel, or even an antique milk can on their porch or lawn is also likely to have collected some other things. Several burglars we interviewed used these exterior signs as predictors for finding some gold coins, stamps, old guns, good silver service, or other collectibles inside. The burglar's logic was that these people were consistent and the valuables inside went along with the things they could see from the street. People who advertise they are collectors in the local weeklies are also advertising that they own stealable property.

One burglar loved Hummel figurines. "Nobody marks them for identification because they're afraid to wreck them, and the things are bought and sold easy at any antique place or flea market. Who's gonna know? If I buy it at a flea market or sell it at a flea market. Nobody can prove anything." Small, transportable, usually found in sets or collections, this kind of collectible is perfect for burglars because it's easily converted to cash and tough to trace.

One burglar, #13, used his own intuitive feelings for the residents' spending habits to guide his site selection. He preferred "older neighborhoods, where people live in the same house a long time. Then, even if they're not rich they spend their money on things, not the house." He sought older, well kept homes rather than newer homes or those with expensive improvements. He was looking for a sense of the conservative in the homeowner — one who saved money and took care of what they owned. He avoided homes that signaled the owner was "mortgaged to the hilt." According to our burglar, these owners spent every penny earned and more on flamboyant flourishes that detracted rather than added to the value of the home. His examples included expensive lawn furniture that didn't go with the house style, above ground pools and large, flashy cars. These people, he reasoned, didn't have enough left over to buy anything worth stealing.

Should we all live in dull, bland homes to be safe from burglary? The answer is no. The key to safety is fitting in. One should maintain a home that blends into the neighborhood rather than one that stands out because it is unusually flamboyant or conservative. The burglar is operating on his feelings. The goal of the homeowner should be to make the burglar feel that this house belongs to someone with a strong sense of community. The house and grounds are maintained to enhance the image of the neighborhood, not to stand out and be apart from the neighbors. We feel an entire neighborhood maintained this way stresses neighborhood cohesion and will force burglars to search for victims elsewhere. Why risk arrest in a neighborhood that looks like the neighbors are looking out for each other when there are so many areas where it is obvious neighbors care little about each other's well being? A neighborhood that looks like it fits together as a unit is a much safer neighborhood than one that looks like it is occupied by strong individualists. The objective is to "belong" rather than "stand out."

These are just a few of the rationales used by residential burglars to choose a house to burglarize. Every individual burglar has his own particular logic and intuition. They all have some idea about the situation of houses, the neighborhood, signs used for visual inspection of a specific house in the neighborhood, and a sense of timing about when the home is likely to be unoccupied. Now that we can choose a house, our attention turns to some of the ways used to get inside.

Getting Inside Without Getting Caught

The first and most important part of the process of getting inside is making sure no one is at home. Burglars almost always take one or more precautions to be certain no one is in the house. They will knock and ring the doorbell even if they believe the house is empty just to be certain. If someone answers the door, most burglars are ready with a stock question to ask to legitimize their presence. Some of these questions are so common that anyone answering the door should report the incident to the police to protect other homes in the area.

The most common question used by the least experienced burglars when their knock is answered is to ask for a fictitious person. They pretend they were given the wrong address, feign confusion and apologize profusely. This type of story is so transparent that no experienced burglar would use it. Syndicated columnist Mike Royko suggests questions like this be answered with "Yes, he is in the kitchen cleaning his hunting rifle. Do you want to speak to him?" (Royko, 1984). This response is sure to befuddle the inexperienced burglar who is stupid enough to use such a rouse. A difficult to detect refinement of this approach is for the burglar to ask directions to a street a couple of blocks away. This sounds legitimate until many less experienced burglars drive away in the wrong direction. If directions are not followed, the resident should alert the police with a description of the person and the car.

A second response to an answered knock on the door is a sales pitch for a small product or solicitation for a charitable organization. These approaches are used by more professional burglars. They may even have printed identification cards. Be wary of any identification printed in business card form. These can be obtained legitimately by anyone. Young burglars often use the guise of collecting money for a local youth group. Sometimes, they make money through contributions when the door is answered. As they grow older, they switch to a sales pitch. Legitimate sales people always have one, usually two product cases. These cases are a real bother to a burglar who wants his hands free to carry stolen items. Be wary of anyone selling anything they are carrying in their pocket.

There are many variations on the sales and donation pitch. One of our burglars liked to pretend to have car problems. He would turn into a driveway of a likely house and raise the hood of his car. If the doorbell was answered, he asked for water for his overheated radiator. He even took the precaution of draining a little fluid from his radiator so that some could be added if necessary. He felt that people are not suspicious of strangers in distress. If you ask for help, people generally give it without question. Car problems also arouse little suspicion in the suburbs. If no one is at home, the house can be burglarized, the hood put down and the burglar can drive away from the scene in minutes. This burglar's biggest problem was residents and neighbors who were amateur mechanics and wanted to look over the engine and help. They are difficult to fool. To minimize this possibility, he works mostly on weekdays during business hours. Again, residents should be observant about their surroundings. An unfamiliar car in a neighbor's drive may be cause for concern.

The best situation for a burglar is to go through their elaborate precautionary process, then grasp the knob, turn it, and find the door unlocked. This is a surprisingly frequent occur-

rence. Many burglars build their careers on the mistaken be-
lief held by residents that "it can't happen here," or "I'll only be
next door for a minute." More than one of the burglars we
talked to burglarized open houses while the residents were in
the backyard doing yardwork. The most expensive alarm is
rendered useless if the door is not locked and the alarm acti-
vated. It takes just several minutes or less for a burglar to walk
through an unlocked door and walk out with valuables and the
priceless memories they may represent.

Another less obvious form of carelessness is to leave the
door of an attached garage open after leaving home in the car.
Once in the garage, the burglar is out of sight and free to work
on entering the house. In one case, a hole was chopped
through the wall to avoid an alarm attached to the door. This is
just an example of the amount of work that can be done in an
enclosed garage or porch without neighbors noticing. However, most of the burglars we interviewed are easily discouraged by a tough lock. With so many opportunities, many
burglars will move on rather than struggle with a dead bolt
lock or tightly secured window in an area where they are exposed to view.

Methods of entry vary considerably and are becoming
more complicated due to the profusion of burglar alarm systems. It is a complicated situation for the burglar because
some houses have alarm systems but do not advertise the fact
with window stickers, while other houses display the window
stickers but in fact have no alarm system. One burglar we
talked to had his own method of determining if a house had an
alarm system. If he suspected the house might have an alarm,
he would leave his car running in front of the house and ring
the doorbell. When no one answered, he would step back and
kick the door in. He is physcially powerful, and looked as
though he could kick in most doors. He would then run to his
car and drive away. Fifteen minutes later he would drive past
the house. If there were no lights on and no police cars or
neighbors present, he would walk through the smashed in door
and burglarize the home.

Most other burglars, though not more successful, were not

as crude in their means of entry. Some of the methods are tried and true techniques that have been used for many years. Doors with small built in windows are easy to enter. Just break out the glass and reach in and down to unlock the door from the inside. Similarly, windows of any kind within arms length of the door are a quick and easy way inside. The best defense in these instances are dead bolt locks that require a key on both sides of the door. The most commonly used technique over the years is to "jimmie" a lock or window. All that is required is a door or window that does not have a burglar proof lock and has a little play or give in it. In the case of a window, the burglar will work the window up and down until the fastener begins to loosen. A screwdriver or prybar might be used for extra leverage. Finally, the fastener loosens and gives way, allowing entry. The best of the burglars that we met (#20) told us the best way to secure a window is the inexpensive method of drilling holes in the sash and placing ten-penny nails in the holes. To him, this simple safeguard is a "pain in the neck, it's not worth the time and trouble" to burglarize the house.

The tool most commonly used to gain entry is a prybar. This is a tool that is flat at one end and curved at the other with claws on each end. These come in various sizes. The flattened end is placed between a door and door frame and the frame is pried away from the door far enough to disengage or break the lock. One of the burglars we interviewed, #8, took the prybar to the extreme. He had a bar of hardened steel made by a machinist friend that was four and one half feet long. With this bar, he and his brother easily broke down doors and quickly entered houses that had been well secured with dead bolt locks. He compared his burglary style to a "commando raid."

Some houses are built with architectural features that are especially inviting to a residential burglar. Two features that come to mind are sliding glass doors and jalousie windows. The glass in louvered windows can be removed piece by piece with a screw-driver. In one case, a burglar entered the same house several times over the course of a year by using this method. The owners of the house and the police could never figure out how the burglar entered the house because he carefully replaced the glass each time he left the house. The method of entry was finally discovered when the burglar was surprised in the act and did not have time to replace all the panes in the window.

The construction of some sliding glass doors makes it very easy to lift them off their tracks with just a screwdriver. This flaw in their construction is even more of a liability because sliding glass doors usually exit onto the most secluded part of the property. This is often a fenced backyard or patio that is out of the line of sight of neighbors to provide privacy. If the area was secure enough and the house some distance from neighbors, one of our burglars (#2) who emphasized working fast, would simply smash out the sliding glass door with a brick. Doors leading to visually obstructed areas should be the most secure, rather than the least secure in the house.

Finally, small basement windows are a means of entering a house often overlooked by homeowners. Although extreme care may be taken in securing the rest of the house, basement windows are often neglected. They are easy for the home-owner to overlook because they seem so inconvenient. Small, high above the basement floor and hidden behind shrubs, basement windows are a favorite means of entry for many residential burglars.

As an aside, it should be clear now how important bushes, shrubs, walls and hedges are to a burglar's efforts to force a window or door without attracting attention. And when several things combine — an overgrown shrub at the door, a weak lock, a predictably unguarded home — it's hard for a burglar to fail.

The Behavior of Burglars Inside the House

Good residential burglars have a well developed plan they follow once inside the home. They do not wander about at random tripping over furniture and looking for valuables. Most have a good idea what they want out of a house and where to find it. Professional burglars take a few precautions to insure their escape before they go after the valuables. First, they decide on a couple of possible escape routes, and then make sure the routes are clear. If they have come in the front door, they will unlock the back door as well. If the doors are locked with double cylinder deadbolts that require a key, a window or two will be cracked open just enough to be opened easily in a hurry. In any case, the first concern of a good burglar is providing alternative routes of escape.

A nighttime burglar we interviewed often worked in homes while the residents were asleep. He simply took the precaution of lining up several breakable glass items, like lamps, along his path of escape. If a resident awoke, he reasoned, the thought of shattering and broken glass on bare feet would cause enough confusion for him to easily escape.

A second concern is "intrusion time." This is because the intrusion time is the time burglars are most vulnerable to capture. It is a time filled with uncertainty. The burglar is in a strange environment with no way of knowing what is going on outside the house, or when someone may come home. For all these reasons, burglars try to minimize as much as possible the amount of time they are actually in the home. This is something every burglar we spoke to agreed with. A time rule often adhered to is no more than five minutes inside, preferably less. If they are out of the house within three minutes of entering, even the fastest response to a silent alarm would not catch the burglar in the house. In the suburbs, it usually takes at least three minutes for the police to arrive on the scene after they receive a call. More time is required if the alarm does not go directly to the police or requires a verification procedure. In most cases, a burglar can beat the response to a silent alarm if he can be out of the house in three minutes.

Burglars must have a careful plan or procedure while in the home to complete a burglary in three to five minutes. Most burglars, after securing escape alternatives, head directly for the master bedroom.

The master bedroom is chosen because it is usually the center of two adult lives. This makes it the place where many valuables are kept. One burglar looked across the table at us and said, "Do you really think I don't know that you keep cash you don't carry around in your top bureau drawer?" He was close enough to make the point. High on the list of things burglars are looking for in the master bedroom are cash; gold and silver jewelry; gems; other valuables; and guns. In short, the master bedroom holds not only the most valuable, but also the most financially liquid of the stealable items in a household.

Often the master bedroom also provides the ideal container for a burglar. This container is your pillow case. It is convenient, easy, and every house has one. It's a good rule not to steal anything that will not fit into a pillow case. Pillow cases are easy to handle, and ideal for the job. It's easy to understand why so many residential burglaries include a missing pillowcase as part of the list of missing property. This practice is so common many refer to these burglars as pillowcase burglars.

Most burglars conserve time by dumping all drawers and jewelry boxes onto the bed rather than carefully searching each one. Closet shelves will be emptied onto the floor. When the burglar is through, the room has been ransacked. Some burglars—a minority—prefer to be very exacting and leave the bedroom and other areas of the house as undisturbed as possible. While it requires a little more time inside the house, it may postpone discovery of the burglary for several days or more. This drastically decreases the chance of being caught. Local police indicate that some victims initially think a valuable piece of jewelry is lost. It may take several more days for enough valuables to turn up missing to convince the victims they were burglarized.

From the bedroom, the burglar turns his attention to the dining area in search of silverware, silver service, candlesticks and other valuables. This requires a matter of seconds. If the burglar feels he has time left he will usually look for a study that may hold a stamp or coin collection. A quick check for household money left in a kitchen desk or pitcher is made on the way out. Many burglars do not bother with the kitchen at all.

At this point, the burglar leaves the house. Often he walks out the front door, with the pillowcase concealed inside a jacket or held tight to his side. Rarely will a pillowcase burglar steal a bulky television set or stereo component. This is a sign that a real amateur was involved. Cash and things easily converted to cash are high priority. A burglar can legitimately buy a new television with stolen cash. "That way," joked #29, "I get a warranty and everything."

If this is the only home the burglar plans to burglarize, it is not uncommon for the burglar to go directly to a fence and convert stolen property into cash. This is especially the case with drug addicts who are living for their daily supply of drugs that only money can buy. Other burglars may return home with the stolen goods. This increases the time they have the stolen property in their possession and their risk of apprehension. In most cases, the stolen property is converted into cash as soon as possible.

Reasons Burglars Are Caught

Very few burglary cases are ever solved. This is unfortunate but very true. They are so common in some suburban areas that the police do not attempt to solve most of those in which the burglar was not caught in the act of burglary. Instead, police effort is spent teaching people anti-crime techniques and taking reports for insurance purposes.

If police do not investigate burglary cases intensively, how are burglars caught, and why are they in prison? We learned that there are two ways burglars get caught. They do something stupid or they have a run of very bad luck somewhere in the burglary process. We were able to learn a lot about each of these ways of getting caught. Apprehension is the one thing every burglar we talked to had in common with their fellow inmates. Many had progressed beyond the amateur stage into a more professional stage where they were less likely to be apprehended. But because of the record built up as amateurs, apprehensions, though less frequent, almost always resulted in conviction and prison.

Burglars apprehended through their own stupidity often did not think through the burglary they were undertaking and missed what should have been a foreseeable problem. Burglaries bungled because the burglar was under the influence of alcohol or drugs and incapable of planning and executing a proper burglary are also included in this group. In some cases, the burglar actually insured his demise by doing something we would consider irrational. The first burglar we interviewed committed a burglary while under the influence of drugs. He chose a house on his own street where he was well known. He did it during the day. He paused to eat lunch in the kitchen, and on the way out started a fire on the porch of the house. Under these circumstances, it would be surprising if he was not arrested at the scene of the crime. The only other thing he could have done to insure his capture would be to put a "burglary in progress" sign on the front door.

Burglar #4 was apprehended under similar circumstances. He went door to door in a townhouse development trying each front door. The police apprehended him when the neighbors observed his behavior and reported it. He confessed to us this was a very embarrassing way to be caught. He was a drug addict at the time, and desperate. The site was chosen randomly as he was on his way to his regular drug supplier. It is very doubtful that either of these burglars would have made such grievous errors of judgment had they not been under the influence of drugs.

A third example of bad judgment was a case of one too many. Burglar #22 was walking home with friends from an evening of roller skating and drinking. They began to brag and dare each other to do daring things. One thing led to another and the episode ended when the drunk burglar was caught in the act of clumsily breaking into the home of a supposedly wealthy family.

There are other examples similar to these. They all involved bad decisions made by burglars under the influence of drugs or alcohol. The individuals did very little thinking. They simply reacted to the situation they perceived at the time.

Not all bad judgments are induced by substance abuse. There were several errors of judgment mentioned during our interviews that resulted in capture. The first was an impulsive daylight burglary of a corner property two blocks from the burglar's home. This was the first mistake, according to Burglar #8. Burglars shouldn't operate where they are well known. The second mistake was not casing the house and grounds carefully. If he had cased the area, he would have seen the electric company employees working in the backyards. From the top of the utility poles, they were able to see the burglar break in. The burglar was caught in the act. What was the appeal of this particular property? "It was a corner house and real big. And I always wanted to break in."

A second example involves Burglar #23 who specialized in weekend evening burglaries when he could rely on residents being away for a length of time. On the spur of the moment, he decided to burglarize an appealing Main Line home on a weekday afternoon. It was a promising target and he just decided to do it. He was caught in the act when the owners came inside from their pool-side nap. This burglar became too confident, broke his own rules, and wound up in prison.

Both of these burglars had successful modus operandi. Both operated almost at will as long as they followed their tried and true routines. While the pattern of their criminal activity may have eventually resulted in their apprehension, the careless variation from their pattern resulted in immediate capture.

Seasoned, experienced burglars are most frequently caught because something unexpected, unforeseen happened. These are burglars who know the ropes — most having been to prison for prior mistakes due to inexperience. What kinds of things happen when a burglar goes wrong?

The example of Burglar #28, the dirt bike burglar from the previous chapter, comes immediately to mind. He did everything right, but could not anticipate the sick teenager upstairs or the nearby brother who arrived in time to catch him.

Some burglars were apprehended because of bad luck with automobiles. The first was a victim of a classic case of a flat tire at the wrong place at the wrong time. After completing a successful burglary, he placed all the stolen items safely out of sight in the trunk of his car. His tire went flat on the closest main highway to the burglary site. First, he took out the jack and closed the trunk to protect the stolen goods from sight while he removed the flat tire. A conscientious state policeman, warning lights flashing, pulled up behind the burglar to offer assistance and warn oncoming traffic.

The patrolman became suspicious when the burglar removed the flat tire but refused to open the trunk to obtain the spare tire. While they were standing beside the road talking around the problem, a call came over the police radio reporting the burglary location. This confirmed the patrolman's suspicions and the burglar was apprehended on suspicion of burglary until a search warrant could be obtained to open the trunk. The stolen goods were then revealed.

Car problems were also the undoing of the most professional burglar we met, #20. It is hard for us to imagine him having some of the problems other burglars had. It is not surprising, then, that his apprehension was not directly related to a burglary. He had stolen an automatic weapon, a machine gun, during one of his burglaries. In fact, he felt it was so valuable that he took it and left the scene as soon as he found it. He liked guns and decided to keep it. He had it in the trunk of his car one night when he was out socializing. On his way home, he was in an automobile accident. He was knocked unconscious and his trunk opened because of the impact of the oncoming car. The officer responding to the call saw the machine gun in the open trunk. The gun led to further questions, search warrants and jail.

Only one burglar was apprehended as the result of a "sting" operation. The fence he sold stolen merchandise to turned out to be a Delaware State Policeman. A simple burglary became very complicated for the burglar. Burglar #5 served time in a federal prison because he transported stolen goods across state lines.

Of all the burglars we met, only one had ever been identified and caught as the result of fingerprints used as evidence. Leaving fingerprints does not seem to be the grave mistake we assume it to be. This popular television theme seems to have very little real impact on burglary. Only one of our burglars was shot on the job. He thought the house was empty when he began to jimmie the window. An elderly woman in her 80's shot Burglar #11 while he was standing there, jimmying the window. He was seriously wounded, but had recovered by the time we met him.

Finally, there is a case that is a combination of poor planning and accident that led to the burglar's apprehension. The burglar entered an unfamiliar housing development and burglarized a house. He did not realize that the development is laid out in winding streets that double back on themselves with only two exits to the main highway. Unknowingly, the burglar proceeded three times to drive past the house he had burglarized without finding his way out of the housing development. A neighbor had noticed him leaving the house. The neighbor recognized the car when it went by as he was talking to the police about the suspicious incident. Usually, professional burglars choose houses either in familiar territory or close to major highways for ease of exit from the area. In this case, the selection was poorly made.

There are many ways of being caught. Each of the burglars we interviewed was convicted for a burglary, but each had committed many. The point we are making is that a well planned burglary is very difficult to stop, especially in sparsely settled suburban communities where a family member is rarely home most of the day. Sound alarms can alert a neighbor if the houses are spaced close together, but few police departments can respond fast enough to catch the burglar. Several of the burglars we talked to were confident they could deactivate an alarm. Techniques included freon to freeze the circuitry. Because of these difficulties, law enforcement officials face an almost impossible task in attempting to solve the burglaries that take place every day in our neighborhoods.

Style

Before we leave the topic of technique completely, there is another aspect of how a burglary is committed that deserves some comment: the spirit or the style in which it is committed. A specific method, kicking in the door for example, always has pretty much the same result. During the course of our interviews, we were struck by the variations in style and energy a single method could assume.

A glassy-eyed drug addict, the second burglar we spoke to, described for us, in monotone, the desperation he felt as he kicked down a door. It was the barrier between his desire and salvation. He had to have money for drugs, and the door was in the way. How different this burglar's style was from the ambitious, devilish #8. For this burglar, kicking in a door was an adventure with great rewards.

Three general attitudes or views of burglary seemed to emerge from our interviews. The first was an ill informed, slovenly approach. "I don't know no better," was how one burglar summed up his burglary career. These burglars were the drug addicts who turned to burglary to support their habit. Some were simply not prepared for life. Poorly educated, raised by low income parents and without ambition, crime became a way of getting by for these burglars. These individuals seemed incapable of deferred gratification and just lived for the day. It should not be surprising that many of these burglars relied on fences to suggest not only sites, but what to steal once they located the site.

For some, burglary was a career decision. It was a way to improve their economic standing. One burglar got his start in burglary to raise additional money to buy Christmas gifts. All of these individuals held jobs at one time. They worked from time to time as orderlies, cooks, and laborers. Some held more skilled positions in a trade. With little possibility for advancement and frequent layoffs, burglary and other forms of crime became a way to earn extra money. It was also quick and easy. Each of the individuals who had this style seemed to accept prison as a necessary evil. It was part of the job. They were able to reflect on their mistakes. Some even described how they would do it differently next time. One burglar, #9, was considering becoming a "stick up man" if he ever committed another crime. Burglary was strictly business for these individuals.

The third style reminded us very much of the "New Army."

These were burglars looking for thrills, chills and excitement. They really relished the challenge of it all. These individuals, like #8, #4, and #23, became burglars because it was more fun and paid a lot better than their jobs. Burglary was their short-cut to the good life. Lavish suites at Atlantic City casinos, fast cars, stereos, and plenty of money to entertain girlfriends were all available to them through burglary. It would take a lot of roofing, building maintenance or electrical work to live as well as these burglars did during the height of their careers.

If these burglars enjoyed the action and the challenge they also enjoyed the short hours. Some of these burglars developed drug and gambling problems after becoming burglars. Conspicuous consumption led to substance abuse and gambling.

What is the rehabilitation potential for these burglars? Some of them are intelligent, capable young men. They have already turned away from careers, not unlike those taught in prison vocational programs, in favor of burglary. They also seem easily seduced by the challenge, big profits and fast life burglary offers.

As we mentioned earlier, there was one burglar who seemed to stand out above the rest. He was perhaps the only burglar we spoke to who belongs to the elite of his profession. He was remarkably intelligent, articulate, and analytical about his career. He was not, as far as we can tell, conspicuous in any way in his private life while a burglar. Subtle and calculating, this type of burglar also knows the value of blending in to the community. We can only compare him to burglars like Bernard Welch. Welch's career is an excellent example of the elite of the burglary profession. It was a random chance occurrence and a grave mistake that resulted in his apprehension.

Bernard Welch was burglarizing the home of noted cardiologist and well known writer, Dr. Michael Halberstam, on December 5, 1980, when the Halberstams unexpectedly arrived home early from the party they were attending. Welch panicked, shot Dr. Halberstam, and then fled on foot. Halberstam and his wife immediately started out for the hospital. Halberstam was driving when he saw Welch running down the street. He swerved the car and struck Welch, hit a tree and then continued to the hospital. Halberstam passed out one block from the hospital, and died the following day of the gunshot wounds.

Washington D.C. Police found Welch on the street where Halberstam had run him over. He was taken to the hospital for treatment and then to jail. The investigation that followed revealed that Welch, age 41, was at the end of a long and prosperous career as a burglar.

He lived an inconspicuous life with his wife and three children in Great Falls, Virginia, a wealthy suburb of Washington. His neighbors believed him a real estate investor. On the night of the Halberstam burglary, Welch was driving a thirty-nine thousand dollar Mercedes Benz. The Fairfax County Police estimated the value of the stolen goods in his home at 4.5 million dollars. His home was sold at a sheriff's sale for $375,000, considered a low price (Haitch, 1983). Further investigation revealed that Welch owned another home in the exclusive Hidden Valley section of Duluth, Minnesota, his wife's home town. This home was valued at over $125,000, and filled with stolen property valued at approximately 1 million dollars (Sheppard, 1980). None of the accounts we reviewed mentioned any prior criminal record for Welch.

For the very best burglars, wealth is the key. They choose whom to burgle and then study how. Site is secondary. Their work involves research about the victim, rather than the search for a site. They describe their work as though it is an engineering problem to be solved. These masters are few and far between, and seldom caught.

Summary and Conclusion

In this chapter, we have described how a residential burglary is planned and executed. We have demonstrated that burglars vary widely in ability, ranging from rank amateur to true professional. Amateur burglars can be stopped by taking a few simple precautions to secure your home. On the other hand, professional burglars can best be avoided by not attracting their attention. Most rich people do not conspicuously display their wealth for good reason.

The best advice we can offer to avoid a residential burglary is to do nothing to attract the attention of the burglar. Be a good neighbor by blending into the neighborhood. This is generally the case if you are friendly with the neighbors for two or three houses on either side of your property. On the other hand, if you don't know your next door neighbor, it may be a sign that you probably are behaving in a manner designed to make your family a victim of crime. Meeting each of your neighbors is the first step to protecting your neighborhood from crime.

CHAPTER V

SUBURBAN HOUSING, LIFESTYLE
AND BURGLARY

THE AMERICAN SUBURBS were built for the traditional American family. This traditional family consisted of a husband who commuted to work, a wife who worked in the home, and 2.5 children who attended excellent suburban schools. This traditional family, living on a tree lined street in a tract house, formed the stereotype of the modern American suburb.

But suburbs, as we noted in Chapter I, are much more diverse than this stereotype. There are both pockets of low income housing and residential areas of great wealth. Inner suburbs of closely packed row homes are hard to distinguish from those of the older central city. Outlying areas are almost pastoral. These areas are often referred to as "gentleman farms," and it is not unusual to see a horse or two grazing on these properties. There is wide diversity within the suburbs. What all suburbs had in common, until recently, was that they were predominantly residential areas.

The stereotypical suburb is most closely identified with the housing developments built after World War II. Prior to the war, most suburban housing was built in a piecemeal fashion. Homes were built almost one at a time as future owners ordered each unit. After the war, whole housing developments were constructed to meet the instant market created by veterans returning to civilian life and starting families. These were single family, detached dwelling units with large lawns. In this setting, a casual lifestyle centered on the nuclear family evolved.

There is little doubt that the suburban lifestyle was considered better than that found in the inner city during this period of development. American ethic stresses the goodness of small town-rural life over life in the inner city. The housing that both reflected and provided this lifestyle was single family, detached and suburban.

The demand for this housing was spurred by deliberate federal policies that subsidized suburban housing. Many returning veterans took advantage of low interest VA mortgages. All home buyers are able to deduct the interest paid on mortgage loans from their income tax. Another less obvious government subsidy was the crash program of highway construction modeled on the German autobahn. At the same time, urban mass transit systems were being neglected, reinforcing negative aspects of urban life. The American government catered to the prevailing values by providing the infrastructure necessary for suburban development.

The families who moved into these developments had a lot of characteristics in common. Most of the post war developments were soon filled with young families. Women who had operated the heavy machines of the war effort were now anxious to return to family life. The entire nation encouraged them to make way for veterans home from the war. It was considered unpatriotic for women to hold industrial jobs while an unemployed veteran needed work. This was also the last pronatalist period in U.S. history. Large families were encouraged, and considered the American way in the postwar period.

These newly suburban families tended to have very local concerns. They were home-oriented rather than community oriented. Their only major community concerns were for good schools and a safe environment. They selected the area to live in by picking their house, not choosing a community. In choosing a house, they were looking for a residence that had several attributes. The home should have easy access to major centers of employment, good schools and privacy from neighbors. In many cases, privacy was insured by back yard fences and ornamental plantings that obstructed view. Good neighbors and good fences went together.

Emphasis was on the home and raising children. The nuclear family was the norm. This emphasis is in sharp contrast to the more contemporary orientation toward career or conspicuous consumption. Part of this change is associated with a changing economic climate. Housing costs rose dramatically in the 1960s and 1970s. The rule of thumb that a house should not cost more than two and one half times gross income changed to two times the gross income of the family. This financial pinch, associated with a relaxed social attitude toward wives working, led to many two career families in the contemporary suburbs.

In spite of the recent trend to political conservatism and an interest in returning to traditional ways, the American suburban family has changed drastically from past patterns. And, it is not likely to return. The two career household is the most important of these changes. It is closely associated with smaller family size and a reduced emphasis placed on the nuclear family as the center of social life. More emphasis is placed on leisure activities outside the home. Witness the phenomenal growth of health spas and physical fitness clubs for both women and men. Rather than an all encompassing focus on the family, greater emphasis is now placed on self-fulfillment and inner happiness in the suburban person. This results in people spending more of their total money and less of their time on housing.

The physical infrastructure built during the postwar period is ill suited for this changing lifestyle. An increasing proportion of the total suburban population no longer lives in standard family households of mother, father and children. There is an increasing number of family units composed of divorced, separated, single and elderly couples whose children are not at home. These residents do not need the four bedroom, two and one half bath, secluded homes of the previous generation. Their major concern is not for privacy and the nuclear family that may not exist in their special case. Instead, there is an increasing concern for a home which is secure when left empty for extended hours of both day and night. The suburbs are still idealized, but seclusion is no longer the goal. Suburban residents who are not members of a traditional nuclear family do not require, and indeed cannot exist safely with high degrees of privacy.

Privacy is desirable when families are home. The price of privacy, though, is high. In the suburbs, privacy is created through plantings and structures that isolate the home from the view of neighbors. A stockade fence around the back yard will insure the privacy of a lawn party, but it also insulates a burglar from view while he carefully removes a sliding glass door or prys open the kitchen window. Privacy creates an unsafe situation, tailored for burglary, when the home is empty and unguarded.

Suburban homes are empty and unguarded more these days because families are smaller and often both parents work outside the home. Homes are also used less, as more leisure time is spent away from the home. This has caused the focus to

shift from the traditional desire for privacy to security. More people place a higher value on the experience gained traveling, leaving their homes unguarded much of the summer. Tennis, golf, bicycle paths, health clubs and discos all compete with the family home for our recreation time. Houses are becoming a place to sleep and a headquarters to dispatch from. Less and less discretionary time in contemporary American suburbs is spent at home.

Two current trends show how homeowners are adapting to these changes. Both seem to rely on urban solutions discarded in the development of the suburbs. The first is a move back to the inner city. This is referred to as gentrification (Holcomb and Beauregard, 1981, pp. 38-39; Henig, 1980). Gentrification finds individuals returning to the inner city places abandoned for the suburbs over the last several generations. They are moving back to row houses, often in historic sections of the city. These houses, by design and by rehabilitation, are relatively safe from crime. Only the front of the house is exposed to the street. Elaborate precautions are taken to protect the entrance, as well as the less accessible rear windows, from crime.

The second trend is the new construction of cluster housing. This is relatively new to the suburbs. These developments are a variation on the urban row house. These clustered units are designed to require minimal maintenance and have small yards requiring little care. Barbeques stand on decks or a porch instead of spacious back lawns. Clustered housing forces suburban neighbors to live side by side again. Neighbors soon become familiar with each other, and the routines of daily life. Community is emphasized rather than privacy.

A variation of the new cluster approach to suburban housing is the "adult community." These are restricted communities built on the outskirts of many suburban areas with residence limited to "young people over forty." Most of these new adult communities have twenty-four hour security that restricts entry to residents and their guests only. These communities provide a safer environment because burglars cannot drive through looking for a site. These communities also have no residents in their most crime prone years (teens and early twenties) because of the age requirement.

Many two-career couples are making adjustments to adapt their living arrangements in the suburbs to their life style. Communities with full time guards are no longer rare because they can protect homes throughout the day without risk of intrusion. Many older suburban communities have responded to this need for security through townwatch programs. Security through these efforts is made tougher because of the architectural slant towards privacy in suburban housing. Post war homes built for family life and privacy now have many drawbacks. They are too large for today's smaller families and too secluded to be completely safe when left unguarded much of the time.

American suburbs will become increasingly segregated by lifestyle and income in the future. Single people will choose inner city homes or suburban singles communities. The elderly, less advantaged, and single parent households will occupy multifamily dwellings such as apartments and condominiums. Many will choose new alternatives such as mobile homes for economic reasons. The dwellings that the traditional middle

class family will continue to occupy will become increasingly available. These are the large suburban family homes. The value and prestige of these homes will likely decline in the future. Americans will continue to become more cosmopolitan and less local in their perspective on life and their community. The role of the home will change as more activities and discretionary time are centered away from the home. Safety and security will become dominant concerns in these homes that are used less.

The most important factor affecting the suburbs in the future will be an increase in the social and economic scale. The spatial extent of the lives of suburban people will continue to expand through technological advances in transportation and communications. The suburbs will come increasingly into the activity spaces of inner city residents attracted to shopping malls and new industry built on suburban open spaces.

The suburbs are no longer isolated upper and middle class areas. We can expect the suburbs to continue to "open up" to an increasingly wide range of uses. Increased awareness and use means increased opportunity for crime. Suburban people will become more concerned with security. They will adapt their homes to changing life styles and compensate for their vulnerabilities. Our concept of the traditional suburb may have to change. At the least, we must think in terms of far greater diversity than we did in the past.

CHAPTER VI

FINAL THOUGHTS

THE SUBURBS will change to reflect changes in our society. While as social scientists we can see these changes coming, we can only wonder how burglars will respond. Some of the burglars we interviewed will not be discouraged by secured housing or restricted housing. They will still take the risks involved because of the challenge or the potential for great financial reward. Many of the individuals we interviewed are very inventive and resourceful.

Of the thirty-one burglars we interviewed, all but two are no longer residents of Delaware County prison. We hope the other twenty-nine have taken their proper place in society, but we doubt it. Burglary is a seductive profession; often too easy and too profitable to give up for a career as a laborer or mechanic.

We both thank them all for the interviews and insights they gave us. But we both have new locks. And when away, our thoughts often turn to our empty homes.

BIBLIOGRAPHY

Abler, R., J.S. Adams and P. Gould (1971). *Spatial Organizations: A Geographer's View of the World* (Englewood Cliffs, NJ: Prentice-Hall).

Adams, J.S. (1969). "Directional Bias in Intra-Urban Migration," *Economic Geography*, Vol. 45, pgs. 302-323.

Angel, S. (1968). *Discouraging Crime Through City Planning* (Berkeley Centre for Planning and Development Research, University of California at Berkeley).

APSCUF Newsletter (1984). "Faculty Grievances," Vol. 10, No. 9, p. 2.

Ashcroft, N. and A.E. Scheflin (1976). *People Space: The Making and Breaking of Human Boundaries* (Garden City, NY: Anchor).

Avio, K.L. and C.S. Clarke (1976). *Property Crime in Canada: An Econometric Study* (Toronto: Univeristy of Toronto Press).

Baldwin, J. (1974). "Social Area Analysis and Studies of Delinquency," *Social Science Research*, Vol. 3, pgs. 151-168.

Ball, J., L. Rosen, J.A. Flueck and E.N. Nurco (1981). "The Criminality of Heroin Addicts: When Addicted and When Off Opiates," in J.A. Inciardi (Ed.), *The Drugs-Crime Connection* (Beverly Hills, CA; Sage), pgs. 39-66.

Bevis, C. and J.B. Nutter (1977). "Changing Street Layouts to Reduce Residential Burglary," Paper read at American Society of Criminology Annual Meeting, Atlanta.

Bissinger, H.G. (1984). "The Incredible Compulsion of Brian Malony," *The Inquirer Magazine*, August 12, pg. 18-27.

Boggs, S.L. (1966) "Urban Crime Patterns," *American Sociological Review*, Vol. 30, pgs. 899-908.

Brantingham, P.L. and P.J. Brantingham (1975). "Residential Burglary and Urban Form," *Urban Studies*, Vol. 12, pgs. 273-284.

Brantingham, P.J. and P.L. Brantingham (1975). "Spatial Patterning of Burglary," *Howard Journal of Penology and Crime Prevention*, Vol. 14, pgs. 11-24.

Brantingham, P.J. and P.L. Brantingham (1977). "Housing Patterns and Burglary in a Medium-Sized American City," in J. Scott and S. Dinitz (Eds.), *Criminal Justice Planning* (NY: Praeger), pgs. 63-74.

Brantingham, P.J. and P.L. Brantingham (1978). "A Theoretical Model of Crime

Site Selection," in M.D. Krohn and R.L. Akers (eds.), *Crime, Law and Sanctions* (Beverly Hills, CA: Sage), pgs. 105-118.

Brantingham, P.J. and P.L. Brantingham (Eds.), (1981) *Environmental Criminology* (Beverly Hills, CA: Sage).

Brantingham, P.J. and P.L. Brantingham (1981) "Notes on the Geometry of Crime," in P.J. Brantingham and P.L. Brantingham (Eds.), *Environmental Criminology* (Beverly Hills, CA: Sage), pgs. 27-54.

Brantingham, P.J., and P.L. Brantingham (1984). *Patterns in Crime* (NY: Macmillan).

Brantingham, P.J., P.L. Brantingham and T. Molumby (1977). "Perceptions of Crime in a Dreadful Enclosure," *Ohio Journal of Science*, Vol. 77, pgs. 256-261.

Burns, D.B. (1967). "How to Protect Your Valuables From Burglars," *Popular Science Monthly*, Vol. 191, pgs. 80-83.

Capone, D. and W.J. Nichols (1976). "Urban Structure and Criminal Mobility," *American Behavioral Scientist*, Vol. 20, pgs. 199-213.

Carlstein, T., D. Parks and N. Thrift (Eds.), (1978). *Human Activity and Time Geography* (NY: John Wiley).

Carr, S. and D. Schissler (1969). "The City as a Trip: Perceptual Selection and Memory in the View from the Road," *Environment and Behavior*, Vol. 1, pgs. 7-36.

Carter, R.L. and K.Q. Hill (1979). *The Criminal's Image of the City* (NY: Pergaman).

Chapin, F.S. (1974). *Human Activity Patterns in the City* (NY: Wiley).

Chapin, F.S. and R.K. Brial (1969). "Human Activity Systems in The Metropolitan United States," *Environment and Behavior*, Vol. 1, pgs. 107-130.

Chapin, F.S. (1978). "Human Time Allocation in the City," in T. Carlstein, D. Parks and N. Thrift (Eds.), *Human Activity and Time Geography*, (NY: Wiley), pgs. 13-26.

Chimbos, P.D. (1973). "A Study of Breaking and Entering Offenses in Northern City, Ontario," *Canadian Journal of Criminology and Corrections*, Vol. 15, pgs. 316-325.

Clarke, R. and T. Hope (Eds.), (1984). *Coping With Burglary* (Boston: Kluwer-Nijhoff).

Cohen, L.E. and D. Cantor (1981). "Residential Burglary in the United States: Lifestyles and Demographic Factors Associated with the Probability," *Journal of Research in Crime and Delinquency*, Vol. 18, No. 1, pgs. 113-127.

Cohen, L.E. and M. Felson (1979). "Social Change and Crime Rate Trends: A Routine Activity Approach," *American Sociological Review*, Vol. 44, No. 4, pgs. 588-608.

Cohen, L.E., M. Felson, and K.C. Land (1980). "Property Crime Rates in the United States: A Macrodynamic Analysis, 1947-77, with ex ante Forecasts for the Mid-1980's," *American Journal of Sociology*, Vol. 86, No. 1, pgs. 90-118.

Conklin, J.E. and E. Bittner (1973). "Burglary in a Suburb," *Criminology*, Vol. 11, Nov. 2, pgs. 206-232.

Cox, K.R. and G. Zannaras (1973). "Designative Perceptions of Macro-Spaces:

Concepts, A Methodology, and Applications," in R.M. Downes and D. Stea (Eds.), *Image and Environment* (Chicago: Aldine), pgs. 162-181.

De Jonge, D. (1962). "Images of Urban Areas: Their Structure and Psychological Foundations," *Journal of the American Institute of Planners*, Vol. 28, pgs. 226-276.

Downes, R.M. and D. Stea (Eds.), (1973). *Image and Environment: Cognitive Mapping and Spatial Behavior* (Chicago: Aldine).

Du Pont, P.S. (1984). "Expanding Sentencing Options: A Governor's Perspective," *NIJ Reports*, No. 186, pgs. 4-8.

Eck, J.E. (1983). *Solving Crimes: The Invention of Burglary and Robbery* (Washington, DC: U.S. Department of Justice).

Engstad, P.A. (1975). "Environmental Opportunities and the Ecology of Crime," in R.A. Silverman and J.J. Teevan, Jr. (Eds.), *Crime in Canadian Society* (Toronto: Butterworth), pgs. 193-211.

Epstein, A. (1970). "In Philadelphia, Odds Against Going to Jail are Good," *The Philadelphia Inquirer*, Section B, Sept. 14, pgs. 1 and 3.

Eskridge, C.W. (1983). "Prediction of Burglary," *Journal of Criminal Justice*, Vol. 11, No. 1, pgs. 67-76.

Federal Bureau of Investigation (1980). *Crime in the United States* (Washington: Government Printing Office).

Ferdinand, T.N. (1970). *Burglary in Auburn, Massachusetts* (Boston: Northeastern University).

Furlong, W.B. (1960). "How to Keep Thieves Out of Your Home," *Good Housekeeping*, Vol. 167, pgs. 63-69.

Gabor, T. (1981). "The Crime Displacement Hypothesis: An Empirical Examination," *Crime and Delinquency*, Vol. 27, No. 3, pgs. 390-404.

Galub, J. (1970). "Burglars Will Get You, If You Don't Watch Out," *American Home*, Vol. 73, pg. 108.

Gettinger, S. (1983). "Intensive Supervision: Can It Rehabilitate Probation?" *Corrections Magazine*, Vol. 9, No. 2, pgs. 6-17.

Golledge, R.G. (1981). "The Geographical Relevance of Some Learning Theories," in K.R. Cox and R.G. Golledge (Eds.), *Behavioral Problems in Geography Revisited* (NY: Methuen), pgs. 43-66.

Golledge, R., V.L. Rivizzigno and A. Spector (1976). "Learning About A City: An Analysis of Multi-Dimensional Scaling," in R. Golledge and G. Rushton (Eds.), *Spatial Choice and Spatial Behavior* (Columbus, Ohio: Ohio State University Press), pgs. 95-116.

Golledge, R. and G. Rushton (Eds.), (1976). *Spatial Choice and Spatial Behavior: Geographic Essays on the Analysis of Preferences and Perceptions* (Columbus, Ohio: Ohio State University Press).

Gould, L. (1969). "The Changing Structure of Property Crime in an Affluent Society," *Social Forces*, Vol. 48, pgs. 50-59.

Hagerstrand, T. (1970). "What About People in Regional Science?" *Papers of the Regional Science Association*, Vol. 24, pgs. 7-21.

Hagerstrand, T. (1975). "Space, Time and Human Conditions," in A. Karlquist, L. Lundquist, and F. Snickars (Eds.), *Dynamic Allocation of Urban Space* (Farnborough: Saxon House), pgs. 3-12.

Haitch, R. (1983). "Sequel to a Slaying," *New York Times*, March 20, p. 45.

Henig, J.R. (1980). "Gentrification and Displacement Within Cities: A Comparative Analysis," *Social Science Quarterly*, Vol. 61, pgs. 638-652.

Hensler, D.A. (1976). "The Structure of Journeys and the Nature of Travel Patterns," *Environment and Planning A*, Vol. 8, pgs. 655-672.

Hindelang, M.J., M. Gottfredson and J. Garofalo (1978). *Victims of Personal Crime* (Cambridge, MA: Ballinger).

Holcomb, B.H. and R. Beauregard (1981). *Revitalizing Cities*, (Washington, DC: Association of American Geographers, Resource Publications in Geography).

Inciardi, J.A. (Ed.) (1981). *The Drugs-Crime Connection* (Beverly Hills: Sage).

Jackson, B. (1969). *A Thief's Primer* (NY: Macmillan).

Jeffrey, M. (1968). *A Burglar's Life* (Sydney: Angus and Robertson).

Larson, E. (1981). "Saga of Joey Coyle," *Wall Street Journal*, May 27, p. 1.

Lesieur, H. and R.L. Custer (1984). "Pathological Gambling: Roots, Phases, and Treatment," *The Annals of the American Academy of Political and Social Science*, Vol. 474, pgs. 146-156.

Letkemann, P. (1973). *Crime as Work* (Englewood Cliffs, NJ: Prentice-Hall).

Ley, D. (1974). *The Black Inner City as Frontier Outpost* (Washington, DC: Association of American Geographers, Monograph No. 7).

Ley, D. and R. Cybriwsky (1974). "Urban Graffiti as Territorial Markers," *Annals of the Association of American Geographers*, Vol. 64, No. 4, pgs. 491-505.

Lowe, J.C. and S. Moryadas (1975). *The Geography of Movement* (Boston: Houghton Mifflin).

Loyd, B.S., J.J. Monk and A.C. Rengert (1982). "Landscapes of the Home," in A.C. Rengert and J.J. Monk (Eds.), *Women and Spatial Change* (NY: Kendall/Hunt), pgs. 3-5.

Luedtke, G. and Associates (1970). Crime and the Physical City: Neighborhood Design Techniques for Crime Prevention (Springfield, VA: National Technical Information Service).

Lynch, K. (1960). *The Image of the City* (Cambridge: MIT Press).

Mazey, M.E. and D.R. Lee (1983). *Her Space, Her Place: A Geography of Women* (Washington, DC: Association of American Geographers).

McNamara, J.D. (1984). *Safe and Sane: The Sensible Way to Protect Yourself, Your Loved Ones, Your Property and Possessions* (NY: Putnam).

Miller, R. (1982). "Household Activity Patterns in Nineteenth-Century Suburbs: A Time Geographic Exploration," *Annals of the Association of American Geographers*, Vol. 72, No. 3, pgs. 355-371.

Molumby, T. (1976). "Patterns of Crime in a University Housing Project," *American Behavioral Scientist*, Vol. 20, 247-259.

Morrill, R. (1965). "The Negro Ghetto: Problems and Alternatives," *Geographical Review*, Vol. 55, pgs. 339-381.

Muller, P.O. (1981). *Contemporary Suburban America* (Englewood Cliffs, NJ: Prentice-Hall).

Palm, R. and A. Pred (1974). "A Time-Geographic Perspective on Problems of Inequality for Women," Berkeley, University of California, Institute of Urban and Regional Development, Working Paper No. 236.

Pennsylvania Department of Community Affairs (1983). Interprise Development Area (Unpublished document).

Phillips, P. (1980). "Characteristics and Typology of the Journey to Crime," in D. Georges-Abeyie and K.D. Harris (Eds.), *Crime: A Spatial Perspective* (NY: Columbia Universtiy Press), pgs. 167-180.

Pipkin, J.S. (1981). "Cognitive Behavioral Geography and Repetitive Travel," in K.R. Cox and R.G. Golledge (Eds.), *Behavioral Problems in Geography Revisited* (NY: Methuen), pgs. 145-181.

Plate, T. (1975). *Crime Pays* (NY: Simon and Schuster).

Pope, C.E. (1975). "Dimensions of Burglary: An Empirical Examination of Offense and Offender Characteristics," Ph.D. diss., School of Criminal Justice, State University of New York, at Albany.

Pope, C.E. (1977). *Crime Specific Analysis: The Characteristics of Burglary Incidents* (Washington, DC: U.S. Department of Justice).

Pred, A. (1981). "Of Paths and Projects: Individual Behavior and Its Societal Context," in K.R. Cox and R.G. Golledge (Eds.), *Behavioral Problems in Geography Revisited* (NY: Methuen), pgs. 231-255.

Pyle, G.F. (1974). *The Spatial Dynamics of Crime* (Chicago: Department of Geography, University of Chicago Research Paper No. 159).

Rengert, G.F. (1975). "Some Effects of Being Female on Criminal Spatial Behavior," *The Pennsylvania Geographer*, Vol. 13, No. 2, pgs. 10-18.

Rengert, G.F. (1980). "Spatial Aspects of Criminal Behavior," in D. Georges-Abeyie and K.D. Harris (Eds.), *Crime: A Spatial Perspective* (NY: Columbia University Press), pgs. 47-57.

Rengert, G.F. and Wasilchick (1980). "Residential Burglary: The Awareness and Use of Extended Space," Paper read at American Society of Criminology Annual Meeting, San Francisco.

Reppetto, T.A. (1974). *Residential Crime* (Cambridge, MA: Ballinger).

Rhodes, W.M., C. Conly and C. Schachter (1980). *The Criminal Commute: A Study of the Geography of Crime and Justice in the District of Columbia* (Washington: Institute for Law and Social Research).

Rosseau, J. (1964). *The Social Contract*, Translated by M. Cranston (Baltimore: Penguin Books).

Royko, M. (1984). *West Chester Daily Local News*, July 27, p. 8.

Scarr, H.A. (1973). *Patterns of Burglary* (Washington, DC: U.S. Government Printing Office).

Shapcott, M. and P. Steadman (1978). "Rhythms of Urban Activity," in T. Carlstein, D. Parks and N. Thrift (Eds.), *Human Activity and Time Geography* (NY: Wiley), pgs. 49-74.

Sheppard, N. (1980). "Authorities Search Home of Suspect," *New York Times*, Dec. 10, p. 21.

Shover, N.E. (1971). "Burglary as an Occupation," Ph.D. diss., University of Illinois at Urbana-Champaign.

Tolman, E.C. (1948). "Cognitive Maps in Rats and Man," *Psychological Review*, Vol. 55, pgs. 189-208.

Trowbridge, C.C. (1913). "Fundamental Methods of Orientation and Imaginary Maps," *Science*, Vol. 39, pgs. 1-6.

U.S. Bureau of Census (1973; 1983). *County Business Patterns* (Washington, DC: U.S. Government Printing Office).

Waller, I. and W. Okihiro (1978). Burglary: *The Victim and the Public* (Toronto: University of Toronto Press).

Walsh, D. (1980). *Breakins: Burglary From Private Homes* (London: Constable).

Whyte, W.H. (1956). *The Organizational Man* (Garden City, NY: Doubleday).

Wiederanders, M. (1983). "Community Time Structuring: An Alternative to Traditional Probation and Parole Supervision," Paper read at American Society of Criminology, Denver.

Vito, G.F., D.R. Longmire and J.P. Kenney (1984). "Burglary Supression: A Review of Program Findings," *Journal of Contemporary Criminal Justice*, Vol. 2, No. 3, pgs. 11-14.

Wolpert, J. (1964). "The Decision Process in Spatial Context," *Annals of the Association of American Geographers*, Vol. 54, pgs. 537-538.

AUTHOR INDEX

A

Adams, J.S., 69

B

Ball, J., 48
Beauregard, R., 108
Bevis, C., 85
Bissinger, H.G., 36, 47
Bittner, E., 21, 47
Brantingham, P.J., 55, 77, 84
Burns, D.B., 30

C

Cantor, D., 61, 66
Carlstein, T., 21
Chapin, F.S., 21, 26, 50, 69
Cohen, L.E., 4, 30, 31, 61, 66
Conklin, J.E., 21, 47

D

du Pont, P.S., 46

E

Epstein, A., 47, 75

F

Felson, M., 4, 30, 31
Flueck, S.A., 48
Furlong, W.B., 30

G

Galub, J., 30
Garofalo, J., 3

Gettinger, S., 44, 45, 46, 51
Gibbs, 41
Golledge, R., 63
Gottfredson, A.M., 3

H

Hagerstrand, T., 21
Haitch, R., 102
Hindelang, M.J., 3
Henig, J., 108
Hansher, D., 63
Holcomb, B., 108

I

Inciardi, J., 47

J

Jackson, B., 4, 47
Jeffery, M., 47

L

Larson, E., 66
Lee, D., 22
Letkemann, P., 41, 48
Ley, D., 62
Loyd, B., 22
Luedtke, G., 85
Lynch, K., 62

M

Mazey, M., 22
Miller, R., 22
Monk, J., 22
Morrill, R., 62

121

Muller, P., 4, 74

N

Nurco, E., 48
Nutter, J., 85

P

Palm, R., 22
Parkes, D., 21
Pipkin, J., 20, 45, 63, 67
Plate, T., 43, 49
Pred, A., 22, 45

R

Reppetto, T., 27, 43, 44, 48, 61
Rengert, A., 22
Rengert, G., 4, 22, 53, 85
Rossen, J.A., 48

Royko, M., 88

S

Scarr, H., 27, 61
Shelly, 41
Shopcott, M., 27, 50
Sheppard, N., 102
Steadmann, P., 27, 50

T

Thrift, N., 21

W

Walsh, D., 4, 20, 30
Wasilchick, J., 4, 85
Whyte, W., 84
Wiederanders, M., 46
Wolpert, J., 54

SUBJECT INDEX

A

Addiction,
    drugs, 41, 43, 44, 47, 48, 54, 101
    gambling, 41, 43, 44, 47, 54
Adult communities, 109
Atlantic City, 36
Awareness space, 55, 59, 74

B

Bala Cynwyd, 29
Birmingham Twp., 12
Blue collar, 12, 13, 62, 74
Breaking and entering, 88-92
British Broadcast Corp., 27
Burglar #2, 92
Burglar #4, 101
Burglar #5, 98
Burglar #8, 91, 97, 100, 101
Burglar #9, 100
Burglar #11, 99
Burglar #12, 44
Burglar #13, 87
Burglar #18, 83
Burglar #20, 91, 98
Burglar #23, 39, 41, 97, 101
Burglar #26, 34
Burglar #28, 36, 38, 39, 97
Burglar #29, 95
Burglar #31, 41
Burglar #34, 41
Burglars
    apprehension of, 95-99
    characteristics of, 7-8
      age, 7

criminal record, 7-8
    education, 7
    employment, 7
    family, 8
    race, 7
    decisions of, 53-54
    opportunistic, 81
    rehabilitation of, 43-48
    residences of, 7, 57-58
Burglary,
    antiques and, 87
    architecture and, 30, 107-111
    casing for, 29, 64
    employment and, 43-48
    planning of, 21, 76-84
    process, 3-4, 6-7
    situational, 53, 57, 65-66, 77
    smash and grab, 33, 77
    style, 99-102

C

Chester, City of, 7, 9, 12, 13, 55, 57
Cluster housing, 109
Concord Twp., 11, 12
Coyle, Joey, 65, 66
Crime displacement, 74-75
Criminal activity space, 55

D

Darby Borough, 7, 11
Darby Twp., 9
Delaware (state), 8
Delaware County, 8, 16, 33, 57, 59, 72
    areas within,
      Bedroom Suburbs, 11-12

Blue Collar Riverfront, 12-13
Main Line, 9-10
characteristics of,
newspapers, 82
population, 9
size, 9
Delaware County Prison, 16, 19
Delaware River, 8, 12, 62
Diffusion of crime, 75
Direction to crime, 68-72
Discretionary time, 21, 22, 23, 45, 56,
108, 111
Discretionary time,
of burglars, 32, 51
Distance to crime, 67

E

Eddystone Borough, 13
Employment, 46, 51

F

Family,
two career, 106-107, 109
Fence, 49, 65, 67, 72, 74, 78, 79, 95, 98
Fingerprints, 98
Folcroft, 11

G

Gambling addiction, 36
Gentrification, 30, 31, 108

H

Habit and spatial learning, 63, 65
Halberstam, Michael, 101, 102
Haverford, 74
Home guardianship, 32
Housekeeper, 51
Housesitter, 51, 83

I

Inside time, 49
(see intrusion time)
Intensive supervision, 45, 46, 48
Georgia, 45, 46, 48
Calif., 46
Delaware, 46
Intrusion time, 20, 32, 49, 93

J

Jalousie windows, 91-92

L

Logic, burglary, 6, 50, 80

M

Marcus Hook Borough, 13, 62
Main Line, 9, 10, 11, 14, 15, 29, 62, 74
Malony, Bryan, 36
Marple Twp., 11, 55
Media Borough, 59
Middle class, 11, 12, 54, 62, 74
Modus operandi, 77, 78, 79, 97
Montgomery County, 10, 62

N

Nether Providence Twp., 11
New Jersey, 8
Newtown Twp., 74
Nondiscretionary time, 21, 22, 23
of burglary, 32

P

Pagans (motorcycle club), 62
Pennsylvania, 8, 9
Pennsylvania Department of Community
Affairs, 13
Pennsylvania Railroad, 9, 12
Penn Wynn, 29
Philadelphia, 8, 9, 47, 49, 57
Pillow case, 78, 94, 95
Prep time, 33, 39
Professional athletes, 49, 66
as targets, 83

R

Radnor Twp., 55, 60, 61, 74
Rationale, burglary, 88
(*see also* Logic)
Rehabilitation of criminals, 32
Rousseau, 51
Route 3, 62

S

Search space, 55, 59

Secondary sources of spatial information, (*see also* fence) 65, 72
Sharon Hill, 7, 11
Site selection, 81-88
Situational crimes, 53, 57, 65, 66, 67, 77, 78
Sliding glass doors, 91-92
Smash and grab, 77
Spatial activity
 criminal and noncriminal
  relationship of, 67-68, 111, 112
  work places and, 68-69, 111
  recreation places and, 69-71, 111
  secondary sources of information and, 72
Spatial awareness, 63
Spatial explorations, 64-67
Spatial information, second hand (*See also* Fence), 72
Spatial learning, 63
 active, 63
 passive, 63-64
 secondary sources of,
  fences, 65, 79
  media, 65
  friends, 65
Spatial perception, 54, 63
Springfield Twp., 11
Sting operation, 98
Street corner planning, 78
Street layout, 84

Style, burglary, 66, 99
Suburban architecture, 30, 86
Suburban lifestyle, 106-107

T

Temple University, 5
Thornbury Twp., 59
Time, 20
Time blocks, 22, 27, 34, 49
Time diary of burglars, 33, 34, 67, 68
Time use,
 criminal's, 32-43
 discretionary, 21-29, 32
 intrusion time, 20-21, 32, 93
 nondiscretionary, 21-29, 32
 "prep" time, 33
 suburban family, 107-108
 victim's, 22-29
Trainer Borough, 13, 62

U

Unemployment, 41, 43
Upper Darby, 7

W

Welch, Bernard, 101, 102
West Chester Pike
 (*see* Route 3)

Y

Yeadon, 9